2017 SQA Past Papers with Answers

National 5
ENGLISH

2015, 2016 & 2017 Exams

HODDER GIBSON
AN HACHETTE UK COMPANY

This book contains the official SQA 2015, 2016 and 2017 Exams for National 5 English, with associated SQA-approved answers modified from the official marking instructions that accompany the paper.

In addition the book contains study skills advice. This advice has been specially commissioned by Hodder Gibson, and has been written by experienced senior teachers and examiners in line with the new National 5 syllabus and assessment outlines. This is not SQA material but has been devised to provide further guidance for National 5 examinations.

Hodder Gibson is grateful to the copyright holders, as credited on the final page of the Answer section, for permission to use their material. Every effort has been made to trace the copyright holders and to obtain their permission for the use of copyright material. Hodder Gibson will be happy to receive information allowing us to rectify any error or omission in future editions.

Hachette UK's policy is to use papers that are natural, renewable and recyclable products and made from wood grown in sustainable forests. The logging and manufacturing processes are expected to conform to the environmental regulations of the country of origin.

Orders: please contact Bookpoint Ltd, 130 Park Drive, Milton Park, Abingdon, Oxon OX14 4SE. Telephone: (44) 01235 827720. Fax: (44) 01235 400454. Lines are open 9.00–5.00, Monday to Saturday, with a 24-hour message answering service. Visit our website at www.hoddereducation.co.uk. Hodder Gibson can be contacted direct on: Tel: 0141 333 4650; Fax: 0141 404 8188; email: hoddergibson@hodder.co.uk

This collection first published in 2017 by
Hodder Gibson, an imprint of Hodder Education,
An Hachette UK Company
211 St Vincent Street
Glasgow G2 5QY

Typeset by Aptara, Inc.

Printed in the UK

A catalogue record for this title is available from the British Library

ISBN: 978-1-5104-2176-9

2 1

2018 2017

MIX
Paper from
responsible sources
FSC™ C104740
FSC
www.fsc.org

Introduction

National 5 English

There have been some changes this year to the Course Specifications for National 5 English, but there are no changes to the exam papers, so these remain current and incredibly useful tools in your revision. The exams contained in this book of Past Papers provide excellent representative exam practice. Using them as part of your revision will help you to learn the vital skills and techniques needed for the exam, and will help you to identify any knowledge gaps you may have, prior to the exam season in May–June.

The course

The National 5 English course aims to enable you to develop the ability to:

- Listen, talk, read and write, as appropriate to purpose, audience and context
- Understand, analyse and evaluate texts, including Scottish texts, in the contexts of literature, language and/or the media
- Create and produce texts, as appropriate to purpose, audience and context, through the application of your knowledge and understanding of language.

How the course is graded

The grade you finally get for National 5 English depends on three things:

- The "Performance – Spoken Language" component, which is assessed in your school or college; this doesn't count towards your final grade, but you must have achieved the minimum requirements in it before you can get a final graded award
- Your Portfolio of Writing – this is submitted in April for marking by SQA and counts for 30% of your final grade
- The two exams you sit in May – that's what this book is all about.

The exams

Reading for Understanding, Analysis and Evaluation

- Exam time: 1 hour
- Total marks: 30
- Weighting in final grade: 30%
- What you have to do: read a passage and answer questions about it.

Critical Reading

- Exam time: 1 hour 30 minutes
- Total marks: 40 (20 for each section)
- Weighting in final grade: 40%
- What you have to do: Section 1: read an extract from one of the Scottish Texts which are set for National 5 and answer questions about it; Section 2: write an essay about a work of literature you have studied during your course.

Reading for Understanding, Analysis and Evaluation

Three important tips to start with

- Since there will usually be a question asking you to summarise some or all of the passage, it is really important to read the whole passage before you even look at the questions. Doing this will give you a chance to get a rough idea of the main ideas in the passage, and you can add to this as you work your way through the questions.
- Pay close attention to the number of marks available for each question and make sure your answer is appropriate to the number of marks. In questions about understanding, you will get 1 mark for each correct point; in questions about language features, you will get 1 mark for an appropriate quotation from the text and 1 mark for a sensible comment on the quotation.
- Some questions tell you to "use your own words". This means you mustn't just copy chunks from the passage – you have to show that you understand what it means by rephrasing it in your own words.

Questions which ask for understanding

- Keep your answers fairly short and pay attention to the number of marks available.

Questions about language features

- This type of question will ask you to comment on features such as Word Choice, Imagery, Sentence Structure and Tone.
- You should pick out a relevant language feature and make a valid comment about its impact. Try to make your comments as specific as possible and avoid vague comments (like "It is a good word to use because it gives me a clear picture of what the writer is saying"). Some hints:

- **Word Choice:** always try to pick a single word or expression and then give its connotations, i.e. what it **suggests**
- **Sentence Structure:** don't just name the feature – try to explain what effect it achieves **in that particular sentence**
- **Imagery:** try to explain what the image means **literally** and then go on to explain what the writer is **suggesting** by using that image
- **Tone** this is always difficult – a good tip is to imagine the sentence or paragraph being read out loud and try to spot how the words or the structure give it a particular tone.

Summary questions

- Make sure you follow the instruction about what it is you are to summarise (the question will be as helpful as possible).
- Stick to the main ideas; avoid unimportant points and never include examples.
- Make sure you earn all the marks available for the question.

Critical Reading

Section 1 – Scottish Text

The most important thing to remember here is that there are two very different types of question to be answered:

- Three or four questions (for a total of 12 marks) which focus entirely on the extract
- One question (for 8 marks) which requires knowledge of the whole text (or of another poem or short story by the same writer).

The first type of question will often ask you to use the same close reading skills you use in the RUAE part of the exam, such as Summary of key points and Analysis of word choice, imagery and sentence structure. The golden rule, however, is always to read each question very carefully and do exactly as instructed.

The last question for 8 marks can be answered **either** in bullet points **or** as a "mini essay". Choose whichever approach you are more comfortable with. Make as many relevant points as you can. If you look at the Marking Guide which is used for this type of question (see page 119), you'll get an idea of how this question is marked and this should help you in your approach.

Final bit of advice for the Scottish Text question: when you see the extract in the exam paper, don't get too confident just because you recognise it (you certainly should recognise it if you've studied properly!). And even if you've answered questions on it before, remember that the questions in the exam are likely to be different, so stay alert.

Section 2 – Critical Essay

A common mistake is to rely too heavily on ideas and whole paragraphs you have used in practice essays and try to use them for the question you have chosen in the exam. The trick is to come to the exam with lots of ideas and thoughts about at least one of the texts you have studied and use these to tackle the question you choose from the exam paper. You mustn't use the exam question as an excuse to trot out an answer you've prepared in advance.

Structure

Every good essay has a structure, but there is no "correct" structure, no magic formula that the examiners are looking for. It's **your** essay, so structure it the way **you** want. As long as you're answering the question all the way through, then you'll be fine.

Relevance

Be relevant to the question **all the time** – not just in the first and last paragraphs.

Central concerns

Try to make sure your essay shows that you have thought about and understood the central concerns of the text, i.e. what it's "about" – the ideas and themes the writer is exploring in the text.

Quotations

In poetry and drama essays, you're expected to quote from the text, but never fall into the trap of learning a handful of quotations and forcing them all into the essay regardless of the question you're answering. In prose essays, quotation is much less important, and you can show your knowledge much more effectively by referring in detail to what happens in key sections of the novel or the short story.

Techniques

You are expected to show some understanding of how various literary techniques work within a text, but simply naming them will not get you marks, and structuring your essay around techniques rather than around relevant ideas in the text is not a good idea.

Good luck!

Remember that the rewards for passing National 5 English are well worth it! Your pass will help you get the future you want for yourself. In the exam, be confident in your own ability. If you're not sure how to answer a question, trust your instincts and just give it a go anyway – keep calm and don't panic! GOOD LUCK!

Study Skills – what you need to know to pass exams!

Pause for thought

Many students might skip quickly through a page like this. After all, we all know how to revise. Do you really though?

Think about this:

"IF YOU ALWAYS DO WHAT YOU ALWAYS DO, YOU WILL ALWAYS GET WHAT YOU HAVE ALWAYS GOT."

Do you like the grades you get? Do you want to do better? If you get full marks in your assessment, then that's great! Change nothing! This section is just to help you get that little bit better than you already are.

There are two main parts to the advice on offer here. The first part highlights fairly obvious things but which are also very important. The second part makes suggestions about revision that you might not have thought about but which WILL help you.

Part 1

DOH! It's so obvious but …

Start revising in good time

Don't leave it until the last minute – this will make you panic.

Make a revision timetable that sets out work time AND play time.

Sleep and eat!

Obvious really, and very helpful. Avoid arguments or stressful things too – even games that wind you up. You need to be fit, awake and focused!

Know your place!

Make sure you know exactly **WHEN and WHERE** your exams are.

Know your enemy!

Make sure you know what to expect in the exam.

How is the paper structured?

How much time is there for each question?

What types of question are involved?

Which topics seem to come up time and time again?

Which topics are your strongest and which are your weakest?

Are all topics compulsory or are there choices?

Learn by DOING!

There is no substitute for past papers and practice papers – they are simply essential! Tackling this collection of papers and answers is exactly the right thing to be doing as your exams approach.

Part 2

People learn in different ways. Some like low light, some bright. Some like early morning, some like evening / night. Some prefer warm, some prefer cold. But everyone uses their BRAIN and the brain works when it is active. Passive learning – sitting gazing at notes – is the most INEFFICIENT way to learn anything. Below you will find tips and ideas for making your revision more effective and maybe even more enjoyable. What follows gets your brain active, and active learning works!

Activity 1 – Stop and review

Step 1

When you have done no more than 5 minutes of revision reading STOP!

Step 2

Write a heading in your own words which sums up the topic you have been revising.

Step 3

Write a summary of what you have revised in no more than two sentences. Don't fool yourself by saying, "I know it, but I cannot put it into words". That just means you don't know it well enough. If you cannot write your summary, revise that section again, knowing that you must write a summary at the end of it. Many of you will have notebooks full of blue/black ink writing. Many of the pages will not be especially attractive or memorable so try to liven them up a bit with colour as you are reviewing and rewriting. **This is a great memory aid, and memory is the most important thing.**

Activity 2 — Use technology!

Why should everything be written down? Have you thought about "mental" maps, diagrams, cartoons and colour to help you learn? And rather than write down notes, why not record your revision material?

What about having a text message revision session with friends? Keep in touch with them to find out how and what they are revising and share ideas and questions.

Why not make a video diary where you tell the camera what you are doing, what you think you have learned and what you still have to do? No one has to see or hear it, but the process of having to organise your thoughts in a formal way to explain something is a very important learning practice.

Be sure to make use of electronic files. You could begin to summarise your class notes. Your typing might be slow, but it will get faster and the typed notes will be easier to read than the scribbles in your class notes. Try to add different fonts and colours to make your work stand out. You can easily Google relevant pictures, cartoons and diagrams which you can copy and paste to make your work more attractive and **MEMORABLE**.

Activity 3 – This is it. Do this and you will know lots!

Step 1

In this task you must be very honest with yourself! Find the SQA syllabus for your subject (www.sqa.org.uk). Look at how it is broken down into main topics called MANDATORY knowledge. That means stuff you MUST know.

Step 2

BEFORE you do ANY revision on this topic, write a list of everything that you already know about the subject. It might be quite a long list but you only need to write it once. It shows you all the information that is already in your long-term memory so you know what parts you do not need to revise!

Step 3

Pick a chapter or section from your book or revision notes. Choose a fairly large section or a whole chapter to get the most out of this activity.

With a buddy, use Skype, Facetime, Twitter or any other communication you have, to play the game "If this is the answer, what is the question?". For example, if you are revising Geography and the answer you provide is "meander", your buddy would have to make up a question like "What is the word that describes a feature of a river where it flows slowly and bends often from side to side?".

Make up 10 "answers" based on the content of the chapter or section you are using. Give this to your buddy to solve while you solve theirs.

Step 4

Construct a wordsearch of at least 10 × 10 squares. You can make it as big as you like but keep it realistic. Work together with a group of friends. Many apps allow you to make wordsearch puzzles online. The words and phrases can go in any direction and phrases can be split. Your puzzle must only contain facts linked to the topic you are revising. Your task is to find 10 bits of information to hide in your puzzle, but you must not repeat information that you used in Step 3. DO NOT show where the words are. Fill up empty squares with random letters. Remember to keep a note of where your answers are hidden but do not show your friends. When you have a complete puzzle, exchange it with a friend to solve each other's puzzle.

Step 5

Now make up 10 questions (not "answers" this time) based on the same chapter used in the previous two tasks. Again, you must find NEW information that you have not yet used. Now it's getting hard to find that new information! Again, give your questions to a friend to answer.

Step 6

As you have been doing the puzzles, your brain has been actively searching for new information. Now write a NEW LIST that contains only the new information you have discovered when doing the puzzles. Your new list is the one to look at repeatedly for short bursts over the next few days. Try to remember more and more of it without looking at it. After a few days, you should be able to add words from your second list to your first list as you increase the information in your long-term memory.

FINALLY! Be inspired...

Make a list of different revision ideas and beside each one write **THINGS I HAVE** tried, **THINGS I WILL** try and **THINGS I MIGHT** try. Don't be scared of trying something new.

And remember – "FAIL TO PREPARE AND PREPARE TO FAIL!"

NATIONAL 5

2015

National Qualifications 2015

X724/75/11

THURSDAY, 14 MAY
9:00 AM – 10:00 AM

English
Reading for Understanding, Analysis and Evaluation

Total marks — 30

Attempt ALL questions.

Write your answers clearly in the answer booklet provided. In the answer booklet you must clearly identify the question number you are attempting.

Use **blue** or **black** ink.

Before leaving the examination room you must give your answer booklet to the Invigilator; if you do not, you may lose all the marks for this paper.

On the spot

If you throw a rat into the middle of a room full of humans, it will instinctively freeze. By becoming completely still, it is more likely to avoid detection. Then, it will dart into a corner of the room, hoping to flee danger. If cornered, however, it will fight. Ferociously.

5 Psychologists call it the fight-flight-freeze response, and it emerged very early in evolution. We know this because it is common to all vertebrates. The response starts in a part of the brain which reacts when an animal is confronted by a threat, and is controlled by the automatic nervous system. This is the same system that manages digestion and respiration, and is independent of conscious will.

10 At the World Cup finals, we were given a neat insight into this deeply ingrained response. The players who took penalties, and the former players who shared their experiences as pundits, talked about "the walk". This is the fearful, solitary journey from the halfway line to the penalty area in preparation for a single moment of truth: the spot-kick.

In the modern world, we rarely face danger head-on. It is not like the good old days when 15 the fight-flight-freeze response was regularly called upon to deal with predators (of both an animal and human kind). Instead, the danger we face today is artificially created: taking an exam, giving a speech, taking a penalty.

The psychological response, however, is the same. As footballers walk towards the spot, they are experiencing precisely the things you experience when put under pressure at 20 work. The threat is not to life or limb, but to ego and livelihood. We fear the consequences of messing up.

There is an acceleration of heart and lung function. There is paling and flushing. There is an inhibition of stomach action, such that digestion almost completely ceases. There is a constriction of blood vessels. There is a freeing up of metabolic energy sources (fat and 25 glycogen). There is a dilation of the pupils and a relaxation of the bladder. Perception narrows. Often, there is shaking.

All of these things are incredibly useful, in the right context. They prime the muscles; they massively increase body strength in preparation for fighting or running. The increased muscle flow and blood pressure means that you become hyper-vigilant. The 30 response is beautifully balanced for a simple reason: it helped our ancestors (and the ancestors of modern-day rats) to survive.

But there is a rather obvious problem. The fight-flight-freeze response is great for fighting, freezing or fleeing, but it is terrible if you have to do something complex, or subtle, or nuanced. When you are taking a penalty, or playing a piano concerto, or 35 marshalling the arguments necessary to pass a difficult interview, it is not helpful to have adrenalin pumping like crazy and perception obliterated by tunnel vision. You need to be calm and composed, but your body is taut, pumped and trembling.

Sports psychology can be thought of as helping performers to manage a response (ie fight, flight, freeze) that has outlived, to a large extent, its usefulness. The players standing in 40 the semi-circle holding hands are virtually motionless. It is a nice metaphor for the freeze response. The walk to the penalty spot is curiously self-conscious. You can almost hear the inner dialogue: "Get out of here, run away! 'But I can't run away. I have to take this thing!' "

How to deal with these responses? One way is with reflection. The next time you give a 45 speech or are doing a job interview, take note of how you feel. Gauge the curious feeling of dread, the desire to run away, the way your heart is beating out of your chest. But do not let this intimidate you; instead, reflect that these are normal reactions and everyone experiences them: even Michael Jordan (a marvel from the free-throw line) and Roger Federer (who always looks unnaturally calm on Centre Court).

50 One of the most creative sports psychologists has found that simply discussing the fight-flight-freeze response has huge therapeutic benefit. It takes the edge off. It makes an otherwise bewildering reaction (what on earth is going on inside me?) into a comprehensible one. To put it another way, the first stage of liberation from the tyranny of pressure is echoing the behaviour of our ancient selves.

55 This, I think, is what top athletes mean when they repeat that otherwise paradoxical saying: "Pressure is not a problem; it is a privilege". Talk to David Beckham, Sebastian Coe or Sir Chris Hoy and they will be perfectly open about their nerves and fear. But they also talk with great pride about facing up to them. They didn't see these human responses as signs of weakness but as opportunities to grow. They created mechanisms
60 (often highly personal ones) to help them through. They seized every opportunity to face danger, and learnt from each experience.

So, here is a piece of (free) advice: if you are given an opportunity to take the equivalent of a penalty, whether at work or anywhere else, grab it. Accept that you will feel uncomfortable, that your stomach will knot and that, at the moment of truth, you will
65 wish to be anywhere else in the world. Think also, as you are about to perform, of the footballers at a World Cup who volunteered to step forward with the weight of a nation's expectations on their shoulders.

Because here is the most revelatory and paradoxical thing of all: if you miss, your life will not end. If you fluff your lines, you won't die. Instead, you will grow, learn and mature.
70 And isn't that what life – whether at home, on the football pitch, or in the office – is ultimately about?

Matthew Syed, in "The Times"

MARKS

Total marks — 30

Attempt ALL Questions

1. Explain fully why the first paragraph (lines 1—4) is an effective opening to the passage as a whole.

   3

2. Look at lines 5—10, and then explain **in your own words** what the writer means when he calls the response "deeply ingrained".

   2

3. Look at lines 14—21, and then explain **in your own words two** aspects of "danger" or "threat" we used to experience in the past, and **two** we face now.

   4

4. Look at lines 22—37, and then summarise, **using your own words** as far as possible, some of the changes in the body which occur with the response.

   You should make **five** key points in your answer.

   5

5. Explain why the sentence "How to deal with these responses?" (line 44) provides an appropriate link at this point in the passage.

   2

6. Look at lines 50—54, and then explain how **two** examples of the writer's **word choice** demonstrate the "benefit" of the response.

   4

7. Look at lines 55—61. Explain what the attitude of top athletes is to pressure, and how **two** examples of the language used make this attitude clear.

   5

8. Look at lines 62—67, and explain fully **using your own words** why the advice to "grab" the opportunity might at first seem strange.

   3

9. Pick an expression from the final paragraph (lines 68—71), and show how it helps to contribute to an effective conclusion to the passage.

   You should refer to an expression or idea from earlier in the article.

   2

[END OF QUESTION PAPER]

[Open out for Questions]

DO NOT WRITE ON THIS PAGE

[BLANK PAGE]

DO NOT WRITE ON THIS PAGE

NATIONAL 5 ENGLISH   14   SQA EXAM PAPER 2015

National Qualifications 2015

X724/75/12

English Critical Reading

THURSDAY, 14 MAY
10:20 AM – 11:50 AM

Total marks — 40

SECTION 1 — Scottish Text — 20 marks

Read an extract from a Scottish text you have previously studied.

Choose ONE text from either

Part A — Drama   Pages 2–7
or
Part B — Prose   Pages 8–17
or
Part C — Poetry   Pages 18–25

Attempt ALL the questions for your chosen text.

SECTION 2 — Critical Essay — 20 marks

Attempt ONE question from the following genres — Drama, Prose, Poetry, Film and Television Drama, or Language.

Your answer must be on a different genre from that chosen in Section 1.

You should spend approximately 45 minutes on each Section.

Write your answers clearly in the answer booklet provided. In the answer booklet you must clearly identify the question number you are attempting.

Use **blue** or **black** ink.

Before leaving the examination room you must give your answer booklet to the Invigilator; if you do not, you may lose all the marks for this paper.

SECTION 1 — SCOTTISH TEXT — 20 marks

PART A — SCOTTISH TEXT — DRAMA

Text 1 — Drama

If you choose this text you may not attempt a question on Drama in Section 2.

Read the extract below and then attempt the following questions.

Bold Girls by Rona Munro

Cassie and Marie are on a piece of waste ground. They are talking about their relationships with men . . .

	MARIE:	I don't know how you coped with all Joe's carry on. I don't. You were the martyr there, Cassie.
5	CASSIE:	It gave me peace.
	MARIE:	No but I couldn't have stood that, just the lying to you, the *lying* to you. I used to say to Michael, "If you go with someone else it'll tear the heart out of me but tell me, just tell me the truth 'cause I'd want to know, I couldn't bear not to know." He never did though. So I never worried.
10	CASSIE:	No.
	MARIE:	Do you know he was like my best friend. Well, sure you're my best friend but if a man can be that kind of friend to you he was to me, could tell each other anything. That's what I miss most. The crack. The *sharing*.
	CASSIE:	Marie . . .
15	MARIE:	What?
	CASSIE:	Aw Jesus I hate this place! (She gets up, kicking the ground)
	MARIE:	We'll get a weekend in Donegal again soon, the three of us and the kids. Sure we could all do with a break.
	CASSIE:	I'm leaving.
20	MARIE:	What?
		Cassie says nothing
		What do you mean you're leaving?
	CASSIE:	Do you know she gives me a tenner before every visit to go up town and buy fruit for them. "Poor Martin" and "poor Joe". That's all she's allowed to give
25		them, all she can spoil them with, fruit, so she wants them to have grapes and melons and things you've never heard of and shapes you wouldn't know how to bite into. I'll bring her home something that looks and smells like the Botanic Gardens and she'll sniff it and stroke it like it was her favourite son himself, 'stead of his dinner . . . And I'll have three or four pounds in my
30		pocket, saved, sure she doesn't have a clue of the price of kiwi fruit. (*Pause*) I've two hundred pounds saved. I'm going, Marie.

MARIE: Going where?

CASSIE: It's desperate, isn't it? Thirty-five years old and she's stealing from her
           mummy's purse. Well I thought about asking the broo for a relocation grant or
35   something you know, but it seems to me all they can offer you is the straight
           swap of one hell hole for another.

MARIE: You talking about a holiday?

CASSIE: I'm talking about getting out of here.

MARIE: Cassie, where could you go with two kids for two hundred pounds?

40   *Cassie says nothing for a moment*

Questions

1. Using your own words as far as possible, summarise what happens in this extract.
   You should make **four** key points.   4

2. Referring closely to the extract, show how **two** aspects of Marie's attitude towards
   men are revealed by the playwright.   4

3. By referring closely to the extract, explain **two** aspects of Cassie's mood. (You may
   refer to word choice, sentence structure and/or stage directions in your answer.)   4

4. Gender is an important theme in this extract. With reference to this extract and
   elsewhere in the play, explain how the theme of gender is explored.   8

[Turn over

OR

Text 2 — Drama

If you choose this text you may not attempt a question on Drama in Section 2.

Read the extract below and then attempt the following questions.

Sailmaker **by Alan Spence**

Extract from Act One

ALEC: Later on I opened the window and looked out across the back courts. The breeze was warm. Everything was the same. It was very ordinary. Nothing had changed. I don't know what I had expected. A sign. Jesus to come walking across the back and tell me everything was all right. A window in the sky to
5   open and God to lean out and say my mother had arrived safe. The sun shone on the grey tenements, on the railings and the middens, on the dustbins and the spilled ashes. It glinted on windows and on bits of broken glass. It was like something I remembered, something from a dream. Across the back, a wee boy was standing, blowing on a mouth-organ, playing the same two notes over
10   and over again.

(*Two notes on mouth organ, repeated, continuing while he talks*)

My mother was dead.

My mother was dead.

The breeze touched my cheek. It scattered the ashes round the midden. It
15   ruffled the clothes of the wee boy standing there, playing his two notes.

Over and over and over.

I looked up at the sky, the clouds moving across. Just for a minute a gap opened up, a wee patch of clear blue.

(*Two notes continuing, then fade*)

20 DAVIE: We better get this place tidied up a bit son. Folk'll be comin back after the funeral.

(*Moves around as he is talking — ALEC remains static*)

As long as ye keep movin it doesnae hit ye. Get the fire goin clean the windaes dust the furniture think about somethin for eatin don't stop keep yerself goin.
25   Sometimes for whole minutes ye can nearly *nearly* forget about it, shove it tae the back ae yer mind. Then maybe yer lookin for somethin and ye turn round tae ask her where it is an ye wonder for a minute where she's got tae and ye think she's through in the room an ye catch yerself thinkin it and it hits ye and ye think Christ this is it this is me for the rest ae ma days.

MARKS

Questions

5. Using your own words as far as possible, summarise the situation facing Alec and Davie in this extract.   2

6. During Alec's speech (lines 1—19), there are references to the weather and the setting. By referring closely to the text, explain how **both** of these are important in this context.   4

7. With close reference to **two** examples of the writer's use of language from lines 20—29, explain how Davie is coping with his situation.   4

8. Look closely at the language used by Alec and Davie in this extract.

    Identify **two** key differences between Alec and Davie in their use(s) of language.   2

9. The relationship between father and son is an important theme in the play.

    With close reference to this extract and elsewhere in the play, show how this theme is explored.   8

[Turn over

OR

Text 3 — Drama

If you choose this text you may not attempt a question on Drama in Section 2.

Read the extract below and then attempt the following questions.

Tally's Blood **by Ann Marie di Mambro**

In this scene Rosinella is getting Lucia ready for her Confirmation.

ROSINELLA:		You look just like a wee bride. I'm telling you this now, Lucia Ianelli, some day I'll give you a wedding, I'll give you a wedding like nobody here has ever seen before.
LUCIA:		(*Enthusiastic*) Just like yours?
5	ROSINELLA:	(*Cagey*) I didn't have much of a wedding, hen. We were awfy poor in they days.
LUCIA:		(*Sympathetic*) Oh, Auntie Rosinella.
ROSINELLA:		No, don't get me wrong. I wouldn't change your Uncle Massimo for any film star. No for Humphrey Bogart, no for Victor Mature. My faither wanted me to marry someone else, you know.
10		
LUCIA:		(*Enjoying it*) He did not.
ROSINELLA:		(*Getting into it*) He did that. Ferdinando. He'd it all fixed up with Ferdinand's faither. He wasn't very good looking, Ferdinand, but all the girls were after him because he had a beautiful big piece of land. That's what it's all about over there, you know. The man's got to have land. So my daddy was that pleased when his daddy picked me. It was all set. Then I met your Uncle Massimo. I must have met him when he was a wean, before him and his faither moved to Scotland, but I don't remember. I'm no kidding you, Lucia, I knew the minute I looked at him that he was for me. He was that handsome.
15		
20		
LUCIA:		(*Disbelief*) My Uncle Massimo?
ROSINELLA:		That was before he put the weight on. And he'd much more hair then and it was shining black. Nero. Nero. Oh, Massimo! Swept me off ma feet he did. Oh hen, I shouldn't be telling you this . . .
25	LUCIA:	(*Desperate to hear the rest*) Oh no, go on, Auntie Rosinella.
ROSINELLA:		Well, I never married Ferdinand. I married your Uncle Massimo instead. That's why I didn't have much of a wedding. (*A beat: she is deciding whether to tell her or not, then does so, with glee.*) We ran away.
LUCIA:		(*Impressed*) You did not!
30	ROSINELLA:	(*Enjoying it now*) We did. You see, in Italy, where we come from anyway, if a boy and a girl stay out together all night, then they must get married. It's true. We planned it and we did it. My faither locked me in my room because I said I wasn't going to marry Ferdinand and your Uncle Massimo came with a ladder and stole me out the window.

MARKS

35 LUCIA: (*Laughing*) He did not!

    ROSINELLA: Without a word of a lie, sure as God is my judge standing here. We just had to spend one night together, on our own. But we had nowhere to go so we hid up a tree. And we could hear them out looking for us, all around the village, calling our names and chapping all the doors. My daddy was
40   screaming and shouting at the top of his voice and calling me for everything. And the next morning the priest rang the bell — (*She mimics the sound*) "Do-ing, Do-ing, Do-ing" — the way he does when someone has died, to let everyone in the village know I'd disgraced my name and brought shame on my whole family. Oh it was lovely, so it was.

Questions

10. Using your own words as far as possible, summarise the story that Rosinella tells Lucia about her wedding to Massimo. You should make **four** key points.   4

11. Referring closely to the extract, explain fully how the stage directions reveal Rosinella's changing thoughts about telling Lucia this story.   4

12. Identify **one** interesting use of tone created in this extract and explain how it is created.   2

13. Even though Rosinella is Italian, her speech shows signs of her having lived in Scotland. Find **two** examples from the passage which indicate this.   2

14. By referring to this extract and to elsewhere in the play, show how the playwright explores romantic relationships.   8

[Turn over

SECTION 1 — SCOTTISH TEXT — 20 marks

PART B — SCOTTISH TEXT — PROSE

Text 1 — Prose

If you choose this text you may not attempt a question on Prose in Section 2.

Read the extract below and then attempt the following questions.

The Cone-Gatherers by Robin Jenkins

In this extract, the brothers are returning to their hut, through the woods. They are being watched by the gamekeeper Duror.

While his brother was moving away shouting, Calum was kneeling by the rabbit. He had seen it done before: grip the ears firmly, stretch the neck, and strike with the side of the hand: so simple was death. But as he touched the long ears, and felt them warm and pulsating with a life not his own, he realised he could not do the rabbit this peculiar
5   kindness; he must leave it to the callous hand or boot of the gamekeeper.

He rose and ran stumbling and whimpering after his brother.

Hidden among the spruces at the edge of the ride, near enough to catch the smell of larch off the cones and to be struck by some of those thrown, stood Duror the gamekeeper, in an icy sweat of hatred, with his gun aimed all the time at the
10   feebleminded hunchback grovelling over the rabbit. To pull the trigger, requiring far less force than to break a rabbit's neck, and then to hear simultaneously the clean report of the gun and the last obscene squeal of the killed dwarf would have been for him, he thought, release too, from the noose of disgust and despair drawn, these past few days, so much tighter.

15   He had waited for over an hour there to see them pass. Every minute had been a purgatory of humiliation: it was as if he was in their service, forced to wait upon them as upon his masters. Yet he hated and despised them far more powerfully than he had liked and respected Sir Colin and Lady Runcie-Campbell. While waiting, he had imagined them in the darkness missing their footing in the tall tree and coming crashing down through
20   the sea of branches to lie dead on the ground. So passionate had been his visualising of that scene, he seemed himself to be standing on the floor of a fantastic sea, with an owl and a herd of deer flitting by as quiet as fish, while the yellow ferns and bronzen brackens at his feet gleamed like seaweed, and the spruce trees swayed above him like submarine monsters.

25   He could have named, item by item, leaf and fruit and branch, the overspreading tree of revulsion in him; but he could not tell the force which made it grow, any more than he could have explained the life in himself, or in the dying rabbit, or in any of the trees about him.

This wood had always been his stronghold and sanctuary; there were many places secret
30   to him where he had been able to fortify his sanity and hope. But now the wood was invaded and defiled; its cleansing and reviving virtues were gone. Into it had crept this hunchback, himself one of nature's freaks, whose abject acceptance of nature, like the whining prostrations of a heathen in front of an idol, had made acceptance no longer possible for Duror himself.

Questions

15. Read lines 1—5.

Using your own words as far as possible, explain what we learn about Calum in the opening lines of this extract.

2

16. Read lines 7—14.

How do any **two** examples of the writer's language convey the strength of Duror's feelings towards Calum?

4

17. Read lines 18—28.

Choose and comment on any **two** examples of the writer's use of imagery in these lines.

4

18. Read lines 29—34.

In your own words, explain how Duror's feelings about the woods have changed since the arrival of the cone-gatherers.

2

19. With close reference to this extract and elsewhere in the novel, show how the character of Calum is presented.

8

[Turn over

OR

Text 2 — Prose

If you choose this text you may not attempt a question on Prose in Section 2.

Read the extract below and then attempt the following questions.

The Testament of Gideon Mack by James Robertson

Nevertheless I continued to lead a double or even triple life for most of my teens. It suited me to do so. The fewer people I crossed, the easier life was. At school — outside the classroom — I could be as coarse-mouthed and broad of accent and disrespectful of authority as any of my peers, although I always remained at the edge of the crowd,
5   careful to avoid serious trouble. But in classes I kept my head down and worked. Others, who didn't have my knack of disguise, were mercilessly taunted and assaulted for being good at schoolwork. I studied hard enough to be successful, so that my teachers had no cause for complaint, but my talent for duplicity enabled me also to avoid being the victim of the bullies. Some of my more academically challenged fellow pupils even admired my
10   fraudulence: it was the kind of thing they couldn't get away with, but I could make life easier for them too by helping out with their homework. I was sleekit and cowardly, even though my name was Gideon.

At home, I maintained an air of piety. Although within myself I had abandoned my faith, I continued to go to church and be the dutiful son of the manse. My hair may have grown
15   longer, and I may have slouched in front of the TV watching *Monty Python* — in comparison with which, had he ever seen it, my father would have found *Batman* a beacon of lucidity and common sense — but that was about the extent of my revolutionary activity. I had hypocrisy down to a fine art.

And so, when my father in his systematic, post-stroke slowness began to instruct me for
20   my first Communion, when I was thirteen, I did not refuse to participate, but went through with the whole business. This was a rigorous undertaking. One of my father's jobs was to prepare others for admission to the Kirk, and indeed throughout the year a trickle of young people came to the manse for this purpose. He didn't let them off easily, I am sure, but turned his fierce eyes on them in search of the light of conviction in theirs; and
25   a few abandoned the process under his interrogation. This flushing out of the unworthy he would have reckoned almost as much of a victory as bringing the chosen few safely into the Kirk. But from his own son he required an even greater commitment.

Think of this: the 107 questions and answers of the Westminster Shorter Catechism, in all their Calvinist glory. You would have to go a long way west and north of Ochtermill in the
30   1970s to find Presbyterians who learned their Shorter Catechism by heart, but I did. I was no Calvinist, the Church of Scotland had long since paid only lip-service to the tenets of the Westminster Confession of Faith, and even my father, old-fashioned in so many ways, had moved some distance from a rigid interpretation of such ideas as election and justification. Yet he used the Catechism to educate me in the Presbyterian faith; and we
35   worked through the questions and answers much as we'd once worked through the detail of our days over the dinner table, as a kind of exercise in pigeon-holing holy information. We dissected and deciphered the nature of God, the nature of mankind, the nature of sin, the nature of faith, the requirements of the ten commandments, the form of the sacraments and the meaning of the Lord's Prayer. "What is prayer?" he would ask me, and
40   I, who had given it up months before, would say, "Prayer is an offering up of our desires to God, for things agreeable to his will, in the name of Christ, with confession of our sins, and thankful acknowledgement of his mercies," and then we would talk about

MARKS

what that meant, and look at the several texts from the Bible that proved the points. And all the while, the many, many hours that this took, the apostate in me was picking holes
45 in the arguments, but saying nothing, and the voluble hypocrite was mending them. I'll say this: the grounding for the ministry I would later have at New College was less thorough than the one I had from my father in his stoury study. We understood each other better then than perhaps we ever did. I wouldn't say there was warmth between us, but there was something like mutual respect. And yet, though I was there with him, a part of
50 me was keeping its distance.

Questions

20. Look at lines 1—18. Using your own words as far as possible, explain what we learn about Gideon's character from these lines You should make **four** key points.   4

21. Look at lines 19—50.

   (a) Show how **two** examples of the writer's use of word choice makes it clear how difficult it was to learn all that was needed for the first Communion.   4

   (b) Show how **one** example of the writer's use of sentence structure makes it clear how much there was to learn.   2

22. Look at lines 44—50. Explain in your own words the effect that this tutoring has on the relationship between Gideon and his father.   2

23. Referring to this extract and elsewhere in the novel, show how the theme of deception is explored.   8

[Turn over

OR

Text 3 — Prose

If you choose this text you may not attempt a question on Prose in Section 2.

Read the extract below and then attempt the following questions.

Kidnapped by Robert Louis Stevenson

In this extract, which is from Chapter 2 of the novel, David Balfour approaches Edinburgh as he seeks out his uncle, Ebenezer Balfour, and the house of Shaws.

Presently after, I came by a house where a shepherd lived, and got a rough direction for the neighbourhood of Cramond; and so, from one to another, worked my way to the westward of the capital by Colinton, till I came out upon the Glasgow road. And there, to my great pleasure and wonder, I beheld a regiment marching to the fifes, every foot in
5 time; an old red-faced general on a grey horse at the one end, and at the other the company of Grenadiers, with their Pope's-hats. The pride of life seemed to mount into my brain at the sight of the redcoats and the hearing of that merry music.

A little farther on, and I was told I was in Cramond parish, and began to substitute in my inquiries the name of the house of Shaws. It was a word that seemed to surprise those of
10 whom I sought my way. At first I thought the plainness of my appearance, in my country habit, and that all dusty from the road, consorted ill with the greatness of the place to which I was bound. But after two, or maybe three, had given me the same look and the same answer, I began to take it in my head there was something strange about the Shaws itself.

15 The better to set this fear at rest, I changed the form of my inquiries; and spying an honest fellow coming along a lane on the shaft of his cart, I asked him if he had ever heard tell of a house they called the house of Shaws.

He stopped his cart and looked at me, like the others.

"Ay," said he. "What for?"

20 "It's a great house?" I asked.

"Doubtless," says he. "The house is a big, muckle house."

"Ay," said I, "but the folk that are in it?"

"Folk?" cried he. "Are ye daft? There's nae folk there — to call folk."

"What?" say I; "not Mr. Ebenezer?"

25 "Oh, ay," says the man, "there's the laird, to be sure, if it's him you're wanting. What'll like be your business, mannie?"

"I was led to think that I would get a situation," I said, looking as modest as I could.

"What?" cries the carter, in so sharp a note that his very horse started; and then, "Well, mannie," he added, "it's nane of my affairs; but ye seem a decent-spoken lad; and if ye'll
30 take a word from me, ye'll keep clear of the Shaws."

The next person I came across was a dapper little man in a beautiful white wig, whom I saw to be a barber on his rounds; and knowing well that barbers were great gossips, I asked him plainly what sort of a man was Mr Balfour of the Shaws.

MARKS

"Hoot, hoot, hoot," said the barber, "nae kind of a man, nae kind of a man at all"; and
35 began to ask me very shrewdly what my business was; but I was more than a match for
him at that, and he went on to his next customer no wiser than he came.

I cannot well describe the blow this dealt to my illusions. The more indistinct the
accusations were, the less I liked them, for they left the wider field to fancy. What kind
of a great house was this, that all the parish should start and stare to be asked the way to
40 it? or what sort of a gentleman, that his ill-fame should be thus current on the wayside?

Questions

24. Using your own words as far as possible, summarise what happens in this extract
from the novel. Make at least **four** key points.   4

25. Look at lines 8—12 ("A little farther on . . . place to which I was bound.").

    Initially, why did David feel he was "surprising" people with his inquiries about
directions to the house of Shaws? You should answer in your own words as far as
possible.   2

26. By referring to an example of the writer's language, explain how the writer
effectively highlights David's mood:

    (a) at the start of the extract (lines 1—7);   3

    (b) at the end of the extract (lines 37—40).   3

27. By referring to this extract and to elsewhere in the novel, show how the character
of David Balfour is developed.   8

[Turn over

OR

Text 4 — Prose

If you choose this text you may not attempt a question on Prose in Section 2.

Read the extract below and then attempt the following questions.

Mother and Son by Iain Crichton Smith

His mind now seemed gradually to be clearing up, and he was beginning to judge his own actions and hers. Everything was clearing up: it was one of his moments. He turned round on his chair from a sudden impulse and looked at her intensely. He had done this very often before, had tried to cow her into submission: but she had always laughed at him.
5 Now however he was looking at her as if he had never seen her before. Her mouth was open and there were little crumbs upon her lower lip. Her face had sharpened itself into a birdlike quickness: she seemed to be pecking at the bread with a sharp beak in the same way as she pecked cruelly at his defences. He found himself considering her as if she were some kind of animal. Detachedly he thought: how can this thing make my life a
10 hell for me? What is she anyway? She's been ill for ten years: that doesn't excuse her. She's breaking me up so that even if she dies I won't be any good for anyone. But what if she's pretending? What if there is nothing wrong with her? At this a rage shook him so great that he flung his half-consumed cigarette in the direction of the fire in an abrupt, savage gesture. Out of the silence he heard a bus roaring past the window, splashing over
15 the puddles. That would be the boys going to town to enjoy themselves. He shivered inside his loneliness and then rage took hold of him again. How he hated her! This time his gaze concentrated itself on her scraggy neck, rising like a hen's out of her plain white nightgown. He watched her chin wagging up and down: it was stained with jam and flecked with one or two crumbs. His sense of loneliness closed round him, so that he felt
20 as if he were on a boat on the limitless ocean, just as his house was on a limitless moorland. There was a calm, unspeaking silence, while the rain beat like a benediction on the roof. He walked over to the bed, took the tray from her as she held it out to him. He had gone in answer to words which he hadn't heard, so hedged was he in his own thoughts.

25 "Remember to clean the tray tomorrow," she said. He walked back with the tray fighting back the anger that swept over him carrying the rubbish and debris of his mind in its wake. He turned back to the bed. His mind was in a turmoil of hate, so that he wanted to smash the cup, smash the furniture, smash the house. He kept his hands clenched, he the puny and unimaginative. He would show her, avenge her insults with his unintelligent
30 hands. There was the bed, there was his mother. He walked over.

Questions

28. From this extract, summarise in your own words as far as possible, the main reasons for John's anger towards his mother. You should make at least **four** key points.

4

29. Look closely at lines 5—14 ("Now however . . . savage gesture.").

    Show how any **two** examples of the writer's use of language contribute to our understanding of John's feelings towards his mother.

4

30. With close reference to lines 14—24 ("Out of . . . his own thoughts."), show how the writer uses language effectively to emphasise John's feelings of loneliness.

2

31. Look at lines 25—30. With reference to **one** example of the writer's use of language, explain how tension is created.

2

32. With close reference to this extract and at least one other story by Iain Crichton Smith, show how a character comes to realise something of importance.

8

[Turn over

OR

Text 5 — Prose

If you choose this text you may not attempt a question on Prose in Section 2.

Read the extract below and then attempt the following questions.

All That Glisters by Anne Donovan

The funeral wis on the Wednesday and the days in between were a blur of folk comin an goin, of makin sandwiches an drinkin mugs of stewed tea, sayin rosaries an pourin oot glasses of whisky for men in overcoats. His body came hame tae the hoose and wis pit in their bedroom. Ma mammy slept in the bed settee in the livin room wi ma Auntie Pauline.

5   *Are you sure that you want tae see him?*

Ah wis sure. Ah couldnae bear the fact we'd never said goodbye and kept goin ower and ower in ma mind whit ah'd have said tae him if ah'd known he wis gonnae die so soon. Ah wis feart as well, right enough. Ah'd never seen a deid body afore, and ah didnae know whit tae expect, but he looked as if he wis asleep, better in fact than he'd
10 looked when he wis alive, his face had mair colour, wis less yella lookin an lined. Ah sat wi him fur a while in the room, no sayin anything, no even thinkin really, just sittin. Ah felt that his goin wis incomplete and ah wanted tae dae sumpn fur him, but that's daft, whit can you dae when sumbdy's deid? Ah wondered if ah should ask ma mammy but she wis that withdrawn intae hersel, so busy wi the arrangements that ah didnae like tae. She
15 still smiled at me but it wis a watery far-away smile and when she kissed me goodnight ah felt she wis haudin me away fae her.

On the Wednesday mornin ah got up early, got dressed and went through tae the kitchen. Ma Auntie Pauline wis sittin at the table havin a cuppa tea and a fag and when she looked up her face froze over.

20 *Whit the hell dae you think you're daein? Go and get changed this minute.*

But these are ma best claes.

You cannae wear red tae a funeral. You have tae show respect fur the deid.

But these were ma daddy's favourites. He said ah looked brilliant in this.

Ah mind his face when ah came intae the room a couple of month ago, after ma
25 mammy'd bought me this outfit fur ma birthday; a red skirt and a zip-up jaicket wi red tights tae match.

You're a sight fur sore eyes, hen.

That sounds horrible, daddy.

He smiled at me.

30 *It disnae mean that, hen, it means you look that nice that you would make sore eyes feel better. Gie's a twirl, princess.*

And ah birled roon on wan leg, laughin.

MARKS

Questions

33. Using your own words as far as possible, summarise what happens in this extract. You should make **four** key points.

4

34. Look at lines 1—3. Explain how the writer uses language to convey the memory of the days before the funeral. You should refer to **two** examples in your answer.

4

35. Look at lines 6—16. Identify **two** ways in which the writer develops a strong sense of narrative voice at this point in the extract.

2

36. Look at lines 17—23. By referring to **one** example, explain fully how the aunt's reaction is shown.

2

37. By referring closely to this extract and to at least one other story by Donovan, show how the theme of relationships is developed.

8

[Turn over

SECTION 1 — SCOTTISH TEXT — 20 marks

PART C — SCOTTISH TEXT — POETRY

Text 1 — Poetry

If you choose this text you may not attempt a question on Poetry in Section 2.

Read the poem below and then attempt the following questions.

***Valentine* by Carol Ann Duffy**

Not a red rose or a satin heart.

I give you an onion.
It is a moon wrapped in brown paper.
It promises light
5 like the careful undressing of love.

Here.
It will blind you with tears
like a lover.
It will make your reflection
10 a wobbling photo of grief.

I am trying to be truthful.

Not a cute card or a kissogram.

I give you an onion.
Its fierce kiss will stay on your lips,
15 possessive and faithful
as we are,
for as long as we are.

Take it.
Its platinum loops shrink to a wedding ring,
20 if you like.
Lethal.
Its scent will cling to your fingers,
cling to your knife.

MARKS

Questions

38. In the opening two lines of the poem some of the main ideas and concerns of the poem come across clearly. Identify **two** of these main ideas or concerns.

2

39. In lines 3—5, show how **two** examples of the poet's use of language suggest a positive side to love.

4

40. In lines 7—17, show how **two** examples of the poet's use of language suggest a negative side to love.

4

41. How effective do you find lines 18—23 as a conclusion to the poem?

Justify your answer with close reference to the text.

2

42. The theme of relationships is important in this poem. With close textual reference, show how this theme is explored in this poem and in at least one other poem you have read by Duffy.

8

[Turn over

OR

Text 2 — Poetry

If you choose this text you may not attempt a question on Poetry in Section 2.

Read the poem below and then attempt the following questions.

Hyena **by Edwin Morgan**

I am waiting for you.
I have been travelling all morning through the bush
and not eaten.
I am lying at the edge of the bush
5　on a dusty path that leads from the burnt-out kraal.
I am panting, it is midday, I found no water-hole.
I am very fierce without food and although my eyes
are screwed to slits against the sun
you must believe I am prepared to spring.

10　What do you think of me?
I have a rough coat like Africa.
I am crafty with dark spots
like the bush-tufted plains of Africa.
I sprawl as a shaggy bundle of gathered energy
15　like Africa sprawling in its waters.
I trot, I lope, I slaver, I am a ranger.
I hunch my shoulders. I eat the dead.

Do you like my song?
When the moon pours hard and cold on the veldt
20　I sing, and I am the slave of darkness.
Over the stone walls and the mud walls and the ruined places
and the owls, the moonlight falls.
I sniff a broken drum. I bristle. My pelt is silver.
I howl my song to the moon — up it goes.
25　Would you meet me there in the waste places?

It is said I am a good match
for a dead lion. I put my muzzle
at his golden flanks, and tear. He
is my golden supper, but my tastes are easy.
30　I have a crowd of fangs, and I use them.
Oh and my tongue — do you like me
when it comes lolling out over my jaw
very long, and I am laughing?
I am not laughing.
35　But I am not snarling either, only
panting in the sun, showing you
what I grip
carrion with.

MARKS

I am waiting
40 for the foot to slide,
for the heart to seize,
for the leaping sinews to go slack,
for the fight to the death to be fought to the death,
for a glazing eye and the rumour of blood.
45 I am crouching in my dry shadows
till you are ready for me.
My place is to pick you clean
and leave your bones to the wind.

Questions

43. Using your own words as far as possible, identify **two** things which you learn about the hyena in stanza one (lines 1—9).

2

44. Explain fully how **two** examples of the poet's use of language in stanza two (lines 10—17) increase your understanding of the hyena.

4

45. By referring closely to **two** examples from stanzas 3 and 4 (lines 18—38), show how the writer uses language to develop a tense, menacing atmosphere.

4

46. How effective do you find the last stanza (lines 39—48) as a conclusion to the poem? Justify your answer with close reference to the text.

2

47. By referring closely to this poem, and to at least **one** other poem by Morgan, show how the writer uses word choice and/or imagery effectively to create a striking visual impression, or scene.

8

[Turn over

OR

Text 3 — Poetry

If you choose this text you may not attempt a question on Poetry in Section 2.

Read the poem below and then attempt the following questions.

***Visiting Hour* by Norman MacCaig**

The hospital smell
combs my nostrils
as they go bobbing along
green and yellow corridors.

5 What seems a corpse
is trundled into a lift and vanishes
heavenward.

I will not feel, I will not
feel, until
10 I have to.

Nurses walk lightly, swiftly,
here and up and down and there,
their slender waists miraculously
carrying their burden
15 of so much pain, so
many deaths, their eyes
still clear after
so many farewells.

Ward 7. She lies
20 in a white cave of forgetfulness.
A withered hand
trembles on its stalk. Eyes move
behind eyelids too heavy
to raise. Into an arm wasted
25 of colour a glass fang is fixed,
not guzzling but giving.
And between her and me
distance shrinks till there is none left
but the distance of pain that neither she nor I
30 can cross.

She smiles a little at this
black figure in her white cave
who clumsily rises
in the round swimming waves of a bell
35 and dizzily goes off, growing fainter,
not smaller, leaving behind only
books that will not be read
and fruitless fruits.

MARKS

Questions

48. Look at lines 1—10. Show how MacCaig feels about his hospital visit, referring to **two** examples of language.

    4

49. Look at lines 11—18. Referring to **two** examples, explain how MacCaig uses poetic techniques to reveal his attitude towards the nurses.

    4

50. Look at lines 19—30. By referring to **two** examples of the poet's use of language, explain how he makes clear the patient's condition.

    4

51. MacCaig often uses imagery in his poems. Referring closely to this poem and at least one other poem by MacCaig, show how he uses imagery effectively.

    8

[Turn over

OR

Text 4 — Poetry

If you choose this text you may not attempt a question on Poetry in Section 2.

Read the poem below and then attempt the following questions.

Divorce by Jackie Kay

I did not promise
to stay with you til death do us part, or
anything like that,
so part I must, and quickly. There are things
5 I cannot suffer
any longer: Mother, you never, ever said
a kind word
or a thank-you for all the tedious chores I have done;
Father, your breath
10 smells like a camel's and gives me the hump;
all you ever say is:
"Are you off in the cream puff, Lady Muck?"
In this day and age?
I would be better off in an orphanage.

15 I want a divorce.
There are parents in the world whose faces turn
up to the light
who speak in the soft murmur of rivers
and never shout.
20 There are parents who stroke their children's cheeks
in the dead of night
and sing in the colourful voices of rainbows,
red to blue.
These parents are not you. I never chose you.
25 You are rough and wild,
I don't want to be your child. All you do is shout
And that's not right.
I will file for divorce in the morning at first light.

Questions

MARKS

52. How does the speaker make it clear that she wants to separate herself from her parents in the first sentence of the poem (lines 1—4)? You may refer to language or ideas in your answer.

2

53. Using your own words as far as possible, summarise the impression the speaker gives of her parents in lines 1—14. You should make **three** clear points in your answer.

3

54. Look at lines 16—23. Explain, with reference to **two** examples of the poet's language, how she makes clear how she imagines other parents to be.

4

55. The poet uses different tones throughout the poem. Identify any **one** use of tone and, by making reference to the text, show how the tone is created.

3

56. With close textual reference, show how the theme of family relationships is explored in this poem, and in at least one other poem by Jackie Kay.

8

[END OF SECTION 1]

[Turn over

SECTION 2 — CRITICAL ESSAY — 20 marks

Attempt ONE question from the following genres — Drama, Prose, Poetry, Film and Television Drama, or Language.

Your answer must be on a different genre from that chosen in Section 1.

You should spend approximately 45 minutes on this Section.

DRAMA

> *Answers to questions on Drama should refer to the text and to such relevant features as characterisation, key scene(s), structure, climax, theme, plot, conflict, setting . . .*

1. Choose a play in which an important character is in conflict with another character or characters in the play, or with herself or himself.

    Describe the conflict and then, by referring to appropriate techniques, go on to explain why the conflict is important to the development of the play as a whole.

2. Choose a play where the playwright explores a theme or issue or concern which you feel is important.

    By referring to appropriate techniques, show how effectively the playwright establishes and explores the theme or issue or concern.

PROSE

> *Answers to questions on Prose should refer to the text and to such relevant features as characterisation, setting, language, key incident(s), climax, turning point, plot, structure, narrative technique, theme, ideas, description . . .*

3. Choose a novel **or** short story in which the writer creates a realistic or convincing character.

    By referring to appropriate techniques, show how the writer creates this character, and say why you find him or her to be realistic or convincing.

4. Choose a novel **or** short story **or** a work of non-fiction which explores a theme which you find interesting.

    By referring to appropriate techniques, show how the writer explores this theme.

POETRY

Answers to questions on Poetry should refer to the text and to such relevant features as word choice, tone, imagery, structure, content, rhythm, rhyme, theme, sound, ideas . . .

5.   Choose a poem in which setting is an important feature.

     By referring to poetic techniques, show how setting contributes to your appreciation of the poem as a whole.

6.   Choose a poem which makes you think more deeply about an aspect of life.

     By referring to poetic techniques, show how the poet explores this aspect of life.

FILM AND TELEVISION DRAMA

Answers to questions on Film and Television Drama should refer to the text and to such relevant features as use of camera, key sequence, characterisation, mise-en-scène, editing, setting, music/sound, special effects, plot, dialogue . . .

7.   Choose a scene or sequence from a film **or** television drama* which creates a particular feeling or emotion.

     By referring to appropriate techniques, explain how the director leads you to feel this way.

8.   Choose a film **or** television drama* which has a character who is admirable and/or unpleasant.

     By referring to appropriate techniques, explain how the character is presented in the film/television drama* as a whole.

* "television drama" includes a single play, a series or a serial.

[Turn over

LANGUAGE

Answers to questions on Language should refer to the text and to such relevant features as register, accent, dialect, slang, jargon, vocabulary, tone, abbreviation . . .

9. Choose an advertisement which aims to persuade you to buy something or to change your behaviour.

   By referring to specific examples, explain how successful the persuasive language is.

10. Consider the differences in spoken or written language between two groups of people who are from different places, or who are different in significant ways.

    By referring to appropriate techniques, explain and evaluate the differences in language use.

[END OF SECTION 2]

[END OF QUESTION PAPER]

NATIONAL 5

2016

National Qualifications 2016

X724/75/11

English
Reading for Understanding, Analysis and Evaluation

THURSDAY, 5 MAY

1:00 PM – 2:00 PM

Total marks — 30

Attempt ALL questions.

Write your answers clearly in the answer booklet provided. In the answer booklet you must clearly identify the question number you are attempting.

Use **blue** or **black** ink.

Before leaving the examination room you must give your answer booklet to the Invigilator; if you do not, you may lose all the marks for this paper.

Can Idina Menzel ever Let It Go?

When the organisers of the 2015 Super Bowl were looking for someone to follow in the footsteps of Diana Ross and Whitney Houston and belt out *The Star-Spangled Banner* in front of a global audience of 160 million, it's not hard to see why they chose Idina Menzel.

5   As the voice of Elsa the ice queen in *Frozen*, the most successful animated film of all time, who sang its ubiquitous Oscar-winning *Let It Go* (more than three million copies sold in America alone), she has a more than passing acquaintance with anthems.

The stratospheric success of *Frozen* — with takings of more than £800 million, it's No 5 in the all-time list of highest-grossing films — has elevated her into a new league.

Now she releases hit Christmas albums, has Broadway shows written for her, tours the
10   world's mega-domes and is having a TV sitcom developed.

Frozen isn't going away, either. She's spoken in the past about the much-mooted sequel but she has clearly been reprimanded by the Disney suits: "Apparently I spoke out of turn. I just assumed that because it was so successful there'd be a sequel, but Disney doesn't have sequels, so it would be a first if there was one."

15   How about the *Frozen* stage show, also much mooted? "I think they're working on that but the Disney people keep things close to their chests." If it happens, would she like to be in it? "Sure, I'd love to. But musicals take years and I'd have to play Elsa's mother, probably!"

What's definitely happening is a six-minute short, *Frozen Fever*, in which Elsa's powers threaten to scupper the birthday of her sister, Anna. "It's fun, really clever," Menzel says.
20   "There's a new song. It's pretty much a group number though." She sounds slightly disappointed.

Frozen Fever did delight both fans and Disney — it was shown in cinemas before Disney's live-action *Cinderella*, which doubtless enjoyed a mighty bump as a result. The studio may be tight-lipped about *Frozen* sequels, but they're certainly happy to milk the
25   commercial opportunities of their icy behemoth.

Whether there is a *Frozen 2* or not, Menzel is now a big star, there to be shot at. When she performed *Let It Go* in Times Square in New York on New Year's Eve she was criticised for failing to hit a high note (to be fair, she was singing in sub-zero temperatures). And though her powerful, stately turn at the Super Bowl received strong reviews, there were
30   still some who noticed the odd flat note.

The unnerving proximity of several dozen hulking American footballers may have had something to do with that. Talking about the time that she sang at the All-Star baseball game, Menzel says: "One thing I underestimated is what a strong presence these athletes have when they're standing on the line right in front of you. They're huge, standing
35   there, and you're this one woman, singing on her own. You forget about the world and the rest of the stadium because they're so . . . daunting."

One woman opposite a squad of men: it's a pertinent image given her associations with *Frozen*, a film that has regularly been touted as a feminist breakthrough. The first Disney animation to be directed (well, co-directed) by a woman, Jennifer Lee, it's quietly
40   revolutionary because, as Menzel says, "the purest love that's being celebrated is between two sisters and not because some Prince Charming is saving the day".

Yes, the two heroines are still doe-eyed and partial to shiny dresses, but their relationship is subtle: Elsa, the conflicted snow sorceress struggling to control her powers; Anna, the devoted younger sister whom she keeps at a distance for fear of turning her into a
45   popsicle. With her grandiose sulks, Elsa has been described as Disney's first emo princess. "She's definitely complicated," Menzel says. "I think that's why it's a successful film, because both women are not stereotypes."

Page two

50 There are parallels with Menzel's own life: she and her younger sister, Cara, had their fair share of "Do you wanna build a snowman?" moments. "She would probably tell you she looks up to me, a lot," Menzel says, rather wincingly.

When *Let It Go* was nominated for Best Song at the Oscars a year ago, it was Cara whom Menzel took as her date. "I didn't think about it — she was the first person I thought of — and then I realised how perfect it was," she says. Sisters representing a film about sisters.

55 *Let It Go* won the Oscar for its writers, but that was rather overshadowed by the moment of weirdness earlier in the evening when, introducing Menzel's performance of the song, John Travolta inexplicably referred to her as "Adele Dazeem".

She nevertheless recognises that Travolta's slip was "one of the greatest mistakes ever — it helped my career, that's for sure." It's one of several references Menzel makes 60 to her career: her conversation is a mix of Broadway-speak ("I try to sing from the heart") and battle-hardened ambition.

She is certainly aware of the value of appearing in "several zeitgeist-y things across different generations: from *Rent* to *Wicked*, *Glee* to *Frozen*". There's a 'through line' between those four, she thinks: they all resonate with young people and "people who are 65 trying to find themselves. I'm proud of that. I'm not sure why that's become the pattern for me — maybe it's because I have as much to learn myself".

Our time is almost up. I'm allowed to ask one more (burning) question. Does she have her own Elsa dress, the must-have wardrobe item for girls across the western world? "No I do not!" she laughs.

70 So she doesn't ever have the urge to indulge her inner ice queen and don the full regalia? "Nah, I don't look that good as a blonde. The waistline, though — that would be fun." Part of me suspects that she'd also quite enjoy ruling over her own wintry kingdom.

Ed Potton, in "The Times"

MARKS

Total marks — 30
Attempt ALL Questions

1. Look at lines 1-6, and then explain **in your own words** why the organisers of the Super Bowl chose Idina Menzel to perform there.

2

2. Look at lines 7-8, and then, by referring to **one** example, explain fully how the writer's use of language makes it clear that Frozen is successful.

2

3. Look at lines 11-25, and then identify, **using your own words** as far as possible, **five** things we learn here about the Disney organisation.

5

4. Look at lines 26-36, and then explain fully how the writer's use of language makes it clear that coping with performing under these circumstances is not easy. You should refer to **two** examples in your answer.

4

5. By referring to the sentence in lines 37-38, explain how it helps to provide a link between the writer's ideas at this point in the passage.

2

6. Look at lines 42-47, and then explain fully how **two** examples of the writer's **word choice** make it clear that Elsa is not just "doe-eyed and partial to shiny dresses".

4

7. Look at lines 51-61, and then explain fully **in your own words** as far as possible why the Oscar evening was so memorable or such a success for Idina Menzel.

2

8. Look at lines 62-69, by referring to **two** examples, explain fully how the writer makes effective use of contrast in these paragraphs. You could refer to sentence structure, tone or word choice.

4

9. Throughout the passage, we are given information and clues about Idina Menzel's personality.

   Using your own words as far as possible, identify **five** things that we learn about her personality from the passage.

5

[END OF QUESTION PAPER]

OPEN OUT FOR QUESTIONS

DO NOT WRITE ON THIS PAGE

[BLANK PAGE]

DO NOT WRITE ON THIS PAGE

National Qualifications 2016

X724/75/12

English
Critical Reading

THURSDAY, 5 MAY

2:20 PM – 3:50 PM

Total marks — 40

SECTION 1 — Scottish Text — 20 marks

Read an extract from a Scottish text you have previously studied.

Choose ONE text from either

Part A — Drama   Pages 2–7

or

Part B — Prose   Pages 8–17

or

Part C — Poetry   Pages 18–25

Attempt ALL the questions for your chosen text.

SECTION 2 — Critical Essay — 20 marks

Attempt ONE question from the following genres — Drama, Prose, Poetry, Film and Television Drama, or Language.

Your answer must be on a different genre from that chosen in Section 1.

You should spend approximately 45 minutes on each Section.

Write your answers clearly in the answer booklet provided. In the answer booklet you must clearly identify the question number you are attempting.

Use **blue** or **black** ink.

Before leaving the examination room you must give your answer booklet to the Invigilator; if you do not, you may lose all the marks for this paper.

SECTION 1 — SCOTTISH TEXT — 20 marks

PART A — SCOTTISH TEXT — DRAMA

Text 1 — Drama

If you choose this text you may not attempt a question on Drama in Section 2.

Read the extract below and then attempt the following questions.

***Bold Girls* by Rona Munro**

Extract from Scene Four (Marie and Deirdre are in Marie's house . . .)

DEIRDRE:	But you'd know. I know you'd look at me and you'd be sure.	
	Marie doesn't turn	
5	*Deirdre gets up and clumsily pulls off her top, drags off the jeans. There are bruises all over her back. She goes to Marie and pushes the clothes in front of her*	
	Here, that's you got everything back.	
	Marie turns, startled, then starts to laugh, hysterically. Deirdre hurls the clothes at her. She snatches the knife out of the chair and waves the blade at Marie. She advances on her slowly	
10	I want the truth out of you. I mean it.	
	Marie backs off a step	
	Tell me!	
	Suddenly Marie flies at her	
MARIE:	Tell you! I'll tell you!	
15	*She wrenches the knife and the picture off the startled Deirdre and smashes and slashes Michael's picture with swift, efficient destructiveness. She looks down at the pieces at her feet for a long moment. She drops the knife on top of them. Her breathing slows. She goes to the kitchen area and comes back with a half-filled rubbish sack and some newspaper. She kneels down and starts to clear up the pieces of the picture*	
20		
	(*Quietly*) Watch your feet on that glass there. (*She wraps the glass and the shredded picture in the newspaper. She wraps the knife as well. She drops both in the rubbish sack and takes it back to the kitchen*)	
	Deirdre has barely moved through all of this, she watches Marie tearfully	
25	*Marie returns from the kitchen, wiping her hands*	
	(*Still quietly*) There. (*She looks at Deirdre*) Those are some bruises you've got.	
	Marie reaches out and touches Deirdre's shoulder	
	Deirdre flinches, then allows the touch	
30	*Marie turns her gently. She looks at her bruised body. Marie touches Deirdre's back*	

MARKS

MARIE: Who did this to you?

DEIRDRE: Just the fella she's got living with her just now.

MARIE: (*Stroking Deirdre's back*) They took the lying head off Michael, didn't you know? Didn't they tell you that story?

35 DEIRDRE: (*Quietly*) Yes. (*She pulls away from Marie*)

            Marie seems to focus on her again

MARIE: Ah God forgive me . . . (*She sways momentarily. She runs her hands over her face*) You should go home. It's late.

            Deirdre doesn't move

40   Here. (*She offers the clothes again*)

            Deirdre shakes her head again

Questions

1. Using your own words as far as possible, summarise what happens in this extract. You should make **three** key points.   **3**

2. Look at the stage directions in lines 1-13.

    By referring to **two** examples, show how the playwright reveals that Marie is emotional in this part of the scene.   **4**

3. Look at lines 15-23.

    Identify **one** of Marie's actions and go on to explain in your own words why this action is surprising.   **2**

4. Think about Deirdre's attitude towards Marie in this extract.

    Identify any aspect of Deirdre's attitude and by referring to **one** example of her dialogue, explain fully how the playwright conveys this aspect of Deirdre's attitude towards Marie.   **3**

5. There are many examples of conflict in this play. By referring to this extract and to elsewhere in the play, show how conflict is an important feature of the play.   **8**

[Turn over

OR

Text 2 — Drama

If you choose this text you may not attempt a question on Drama in Section 2.

Read the extract below and then attempt the following questions.

Sailmaker **by Alan Spence**

ALEC: How come ye chucked yer trade?

DAVIE: It chucked me! The chandlers ah worked for shut doon. Ah got laid off. That was it. Nothin else doin. Nae work. Naebody needs sailmakers these days.

ALEC: (*Holds up yacht*) Could ye make me a sail for this? Ah found it in the Glory
5   Hole tae. Ah thought ye could fix it up.

DAVIE: Oh aye. It's a beauty, eh? Be nice, aw rigged out.

           Can sail it in the park.

           Course, it'll take time. Materials'll be dear. But ah'll see what ah can do.

ALEC: When?

10   DAVIE: Wait and see. (*Hands back yacht*) Who knows? Maybe ma coupon'll come up this week!

ALEC: Remember the last time ye won?

DAVIE: First dividend. Two quid!

           Ah didnae let it go tae ma head mind! Didnae chuck ma job. Didnae buy a villa
15   in the south of France. Ah think every second game was a draw that week! Never mind. Some ae these days.

           (*DAVIE sits down, takes newspaper and scrap of paper from his briefcase, writes*)

           Ah didnae bring in anythin for tea. D'ye fancy nippin doon tae the chippy, gettin a coupla fish suppers?

20   ALEC: Awright.

           (*DAVIE hands him money*)

           Can ah get a pickle?

DAVIE: Get anythin ye like. Here's somethin else ye can do for me.

           Themorra at dinnertime. Take this line to the bookie.

25   ALEC: Och da!

DAVIE: Whit's the matter?

ALEC: It's just that . . . ah don't like that bookie. He's creepy.

DAVIE: Away ye go!

ALEC: An that back close where he has his pitch is aw horrible an smelly.

MARKS

30 DAVIE: (*Waves his line*) But this could be worth a fortune! Three doubles, a treble, an accumulator. If it comes up we're laughin.

Here son, ah'll leave it here wi the money inside it.

ALEC: (*Picks up line, reads it*) Why d'ye always write Mainsail at the bottom ae yer line?

35 DAVIE: That's what ye call a nom-de-plume. The bettin's illegal ye see. The bookie gets done fae time tae time. An if you put yer real name on the line, the polis might book you as well. So ye use a made-up name.

ALEC: Mainsail.

Questions

6. Using your own words as far as possible, explain how Davie is shown to be struggling in his role as a father throughout this extract. You should make **four** key points.   4

7. Look at lines 2–3 and lines 10–16.

By referring to **two** examples from these lines, show how different aspects of Davie's mood are revealed by the playwright.   4

8. Look at lines 33–38.

(a) Using your own words as far as possible, explain why Davie needed to use a false name (nom-de-plume).   2

(b) Explain what **two** things Davie's choice of false name (nom-de-plume) reveals about him.   2

9. By referring to this extract and to elsewhere in the play, show how the yacht is used as an important symbol.   8

[Turn over

OR

Text 3 — Drama

If you choose this text you may not attempt a question on Drama in Section 2.

Read the extract below and then attempt the following questions.

Tally's Blood by Ann Marie di Mambro

	BRIDGET:	I knew you'd try to split them up. I warned our Hughie, but I never knew the lengths you'd go to.
	ROSINELLA:	What you talking about?
5	BRIDGET:	You sent her back, didn't you? Didn't care who gets hurt. After all these years you sent her away.
	ROSINELLA:	Who?
	BRIDGET:	Lucia. Who else?
	ROSINELLA:	Send Lucia away? Me?
	BRIDGET:	Well, you did it to me, but you're no getting doing it to my brother.
10	ROSINELLA:	I don't want to hear any more. What did I ever do to you?
	BRIDGET:	What did you do to me? You told me Franco didn't love me. You made me believe I was nothing to him — just a wee Scottish tart for him to practise on.
	ROSINELLA:	In God's name, Bridget, that's all in the past.
15	BRIDGET:	To you maybe. But there's no a day goes past that it's no with me. Franco loved me. Franco loved me.
	ROSINELLA:	Franco's dead — and may God forgive you, lady, for dragging his name through the mud.

This remark knocks BRIDGET off her guard and ROSINELLA gathers her
20 *strength.*

	ROSINELLA:	Now, I didn't want this fight with you, and I don't have to explain nothing to you. But just you hear this. I didn't send Lucia away, I could just as easily tear out my own heart. But I'm no sorry she's away from your brother. I cannie deny it. No harm to the boy. I've nothing against him. OK?
25		Now that's it finished. We'll forget this conversation ever took place.
	BRIDGET:	As easy as that.
	ROSINELLA:	Yes.
	BRIDGET:	All forgotten.
	ROSINELLA:	I'll never mention it again.
30	BRIDGET:	If you knew the damage you've caused.
	ROSINELLA:	(*Angry*) That's it. I've had enough. I don't have to stand here and listen to this. You think I'm not suffering? Lucia's more than a niece to me, more than somebody else's lassie that I brought up and grew to love. She's like the child I could never have.
35		*Silence: BRIDGET thinks, then decides.*

MARKS

BRIDGET: The child you never had, eh, Mrs Pedreschi? What about the child I never had?

ROSINELLA: (*Dismissive*) What you going on about now?

BRIDGET: Do you remember that night, I came to see you? I was pregnant.

40   *ROSINELLA shakes her head.*

ROSINELLA: What you saying?

BRIDGET: I was pregnant and it was Franco's baby.

ROSINELLA backs off in disbelief.

Questions

10. Using your own words as far as possible, summarise what happens in the extract. You should make **four** key points.   4

11. Look at lines 11–16.

Show how both word choice **and** sentence structure are used to reveal Bridget's feelings.   4

12. With reference to **two** examples from the extract show how Rosinella's attitude towards Bridget develops.   4

13. By referring to this extract and to elsewhere in the play, show how the playwright explores family relationships.   8

[Turn over

SECTION 1 — SCOTTISH TEXT — 20 marks

PART B — SCOTTISH TEXT — PROSE

Text 1 — Prose

If you choose this text you may not attempt a question on Prose in Section 2.

Read the extract below and then attempt the following questions.

The Cone-Gatherers by Robin Jenkins

In this extract, Roderick has decided to take some cake to the cone-gatherers, but encounters Duror in the wood.

Peeping through the yew needles, Roderick saw in imagination the door of the hut open, and the cone-gatherers come out, the tall one who slightly limped and always frowned, and the small one who stooped and smiled. Then in the cypress the gun cracked, and the two men lay dead on the grass.

5   It was while he was imagining Duror come stalking out to gloat over the corpses that the idea took root in the boy's mind that perhaps it was Duror himself who was dead. That idea sprouted. Duror had been strolling through the wood, had felt a pain at his heart, and had clutched at the cypress to keep from falling; there he had died, and the green bony arms were propping him up.

10   To Roderick, growing in a time of universal war, distant human death was a commonplace: he had listened to many wireless estimates of enemies killed and had loyally been pleased. Only once, when his grandfather died, had death appeared to him as a tyrant, snatching ruthlessly away what he loved, putting darkness and terror in its place, and at random moments, even in the middle of the night when the rest of the house slept, creating fragments of joy only to

15   annihilate them thereafter. Now the thought of Duror standing dead among the branches of the evergreen brought no hope, but rather began to infect the whole visible world with a sense of loss and desolation and fear. Every single leaf was polluted; even a tiny black beetle close to his head represented the vast tyranny. It was as if all the far off deaths he had rejoiced at were now gathering here around the yew trees to be revenged. Yet was not Duror

20   evil, and if evil died did not goodness triumph? Why then were all the birds not singing, and why did the sun not begin to shine again with morning splendour, and why, above all, was the hut now in shadow? Unable to answer those questions, the boy knelt in an unhappiness too profound and violent for tears or prayer; its only outward signs were paleness and the extra prominence of his teeth.

25   When at last, in the gloaming, Duror moved, it was to the stricken boy like a resurrection, darkening incomprehension and deepening despair. From the arms of the tree Duror stepped forth, and stood for a minute in the clearing in front of the hut. It was a minute of cessation. Incalculable in thought or feeling, gigantic in horror, as if indeed newly come from the dead, Duror merely stood. Then, without any interpretable gesture, and

30   without a sound, he turned and vanished among the trees, as if this time forever.

Questions

14. Look at lines 1-9.

Explain how the writer uses **two** examples of language in these lines to describe what Roderick imagines.

4

15. Using your own words as far as possible, explain **two** different ways in which Roderick thinks of death in lines 10-19.

2

16. Explain how the writer uses **two** examples of language to create a frightening atmosphere in lines 17-24.

4

17. Look at the final sentence of the extract ("Then . . . forever."). By referring to **one** example of word choice, explain how the writer makes Duror's actions appear dramatic.

2

18. With reference to the extract and to elsewhere in the novel, show how war is an important feature of the novel.

8

[Turn over

OR

Text 2 — Prose

If you choose this text you may not attempt a question on Prose in Section 2.

Read the extract below and then attempt the following questions.

The Testament of Gideon Mack by James Robertson

The following extract is from the prologue. The editor has just described Gideon Mack's fall into the Black Jaws.

However, three days after this incident, while the community was still coming to terms with its loss, the body of Mr Mack was found washed up on the bank of the Keldo a short distance downstream of the Black Jaws. Not only had the water apparently carried him through its unknown course, but, even more amazingly, he was alive, and without a broken bone in his
5　body. True, he was badly battered, he had a large bruise on the side of his head, and his right leg had sustained some kind of internal damage which left him with a severe limp, but he had somehow survived three nights outdoors and a subterranean journey that no creature, except a fish, could have been expected to survive. He was taken to hospital in Dundee, where he remained unconscious but stable for a day and a half. When he came round he astonished
10　medical staff by making such a speedy recovery that less than a week after the accident he was discharged and sent home.

Back in Monimaskit, Mr Mack convalesced at his manse and seemed in no great hurry to resume his pastoral duties. It was at this time that he began to talk to some people of his experience. He claimed that he had been rescued from the river by a stranger, a man
15　inhabiting the caverns through which he said it passed, and that he had been looked after by this individual. This seemed improbable enough, but Mr Mack went on to assert that this person was none other than the Devil, and that they had had several long conversations in the course of the three days. These remarks were taken by the minister's friends as indication of a severe shock to his system, and possibly of damage to the brain
20　sustained during his ordeal. Others, however, were less concerned with his health than with the injury his words might do to the good name of the Church of Scotland.

A few days later, Mr Mack, despite his seeming physical and mental frailty, insisted on taking the funeral service of an old friend, an inhabitant of Monimaskit, conducting the event in a way which some considered not just unorthodox and irreverent, but
25　incompatible with the role of a Church of Scotland minister. After the interment he publicly repeated his story that he had met and conversed with the Devil. Finally, at the gathering in the church hall which followed, he made declarations of such a scandalous nature that the Monimaskit Kirk Session had no option but to refer the matter to the local Presbytery.

30　The procedures of the Presbyterian court system are complex, but need not long detain us.　Presbytery, having heard the evidence, invited Mr Mack to defend himself. He admitted the truth of the allegations made against him, but denied that he had committed any offence. Presbytery decided to suspend him forthwith pending further investigation and consultation with the Church's legal advisers, until such time as Mr Mack
35　could be brought before a committee of Presbytery for trial. A libel was drawn up and served on him, but no date had been set for the case to be heard when Mr Mack's disappearance brought all proceedings to a halt.

Questions

19. Using your own words as far as possible, summarise the main events that followed Gideon Mack's accident, as described in this extract. You should make **four** key points in your answer.

4

20. Look at lines 1-11.

    By referring to **two** examples, explain how the writer uses language to suggest that Gideon's story may be untrue.

4

21. Look at lines 12-29.

    Explain how **two** examples of language are used to describe Gideon's character after the accident.

4

22. With reference to this extract and to elsewhere in the novel, show how an important theme is developed.

8

[Turn over

OR

Text 3 — Prose

If you choose this text you may not attempt a question on Prose in Section 2.

Read the extract below and then attempt the following questions.

Kidnapped **by Robert Louis Stevenson**

In this extract David Balfour has arrived at the house of Shaws where his uncle Ebenezer lives. Ebenezer has asked David to fetch a chest of family papers from the stair-tower.

It was so dark inside, it seemed a body could scarce breathe; but I pushed out with foot and hand, and presently struck the wall with the one, and the lowermost round of the stair with the other. The wall, by the touch, was of fine hewn stone; the steps too, though somewhat steep and narrow, were of polished mason-work, and regular and solid under
5   foot. Minding my uncle's word about the banisters, I kept close to the tower side, and felt my way in the pitch darkness with a beating heart.

The house of Shaws stood some five full storeys high, not counting lofts. Well, as I advanced, it seemed to me the stair grew airier and a thought more lightsome; and I was wondering what might be the cause of this change, when a second blink of the summer lightning came and
10   went. If I did not cry out, it was because fear had me by the throat; and if I did not fall, it was more by Heaven's mercy than my own strength. It was not only that the flash shone in on every side through breaches in the wall, so that I seemed to be clambering aloft upon an open scaffold, but the same passing brightness showed me the steps were of unequal length, and that one of my feet rested that moment within two inches of the well.

15   This was the grand stair! I thought; and with the thought, a gust of a kind of angry courage came into my heart. My uncle had sent me here, certainly to run great risks, perhaps to die. I swore I would settle that 'perhaps', if I should break my neck for it; got me down upon my hands and knees; and as slowly as a snail, feeling before me every inch, and testing the solidity of every stone, I continued to ascend the stair. The darkness, by
20   contrast with the flash, appeared to have redoubled; nor was that all, for my ears were now troubled and my mind confounded by a great stir of bats in the top part of the tower, and the foul beasts, flying downwards, sometimes beat about my face and body.

The tower, I should have said, was square; and in every corner the step was made of a great stone of a different shape, to join the flights. Well, I had come close to one of these
25   turns, when, feeling forward as usual, my hand slipped upon an edge and found nothing but emptiness beyond it. The stair had been carried no higher: to set a stranger mounting it in the darkness was to send him straight to his death; and (although, thanks to the lightning and my own precautions, I was safe enough) the mere thought of the peril in which I might have stood, and the dreadful height I might have fallen from, brought out
30   the sweat upon my body and relaxed my joints.

But I knew what I wanted now, and turned and groped my way down again, with a wonderful anger in my heart. About half-way down, the wind sprang up in a clap and shook the tower, and died again; the rain followed; and before I had reached the ground level it fell in buckets. I put out my head into the storm, and looked along towards the kitchen. The door, which I had shut
35   behind me when I left, now stood open, and shed a little glimmer of light; and I thought I could see a figure standing in the rain, quite still, like a man hearkening. And then there came a blinding flash, which showed me my uncle plainly, just where I had fancied him to stand; and hard upon the heels of it, a great tow-row of thunder.

Questions

23. Look at lines 1-6.

     By referring to **two** examples from these lines, explain how the writer creates a sense of fear and/or uncertainty.

     4

24. Look at lines 15-16.

     Using your own words as far as possible, explain what David suddenly realises at this point in the extract and how this affects his mood.

     2

25. Look at lines 23-38.

     Using your own words as far as possible, summarise the remainder of David's journey.

     You should make **four** key points.

     4

26. Look at lines 31-38.

     Explain how any **one** example of the writer's use of language in these lines contributes to the vivid description of the storm.

     2

27. With reference to this extract and to elsewhere in the novel, show how the writer uses drama and/or tension to create a powerful adventure story.

     8

[Turn over

OR

Text 4 — Prose

If you choose this text you may not attempt a question on Prose in Section 2.

Read the extract below and then attempt the following questions.

The Painter by Iain Crichton Smith

The narrator is describing a fight in the village.

But that was not what I meant to tell since the fight in itself, though unpleasant, was not evil. No, as I stood in the ring with the others, excited and horrified, I saw on the edge of the ring young William with his paint-brush and canvas and easel painting the fight. He was sitting comfortably on a chair which he had taken with him and there was no
5   expression on his face at all but a cold clear intensity which bothered me. It seemed in a strange way as if we were asleep. As the scythes swung to and fro, as the faces of the antagonists became more and more contorted in the fury of battle, as their cheeks were suffused with blood and rage, and their teeth were drawn back in a snarl, he sat there painting the battle, nor at any time did he make any attempt to pull his chair back from
10 the arena where they were engaged.

I cannot explain to you the feelings that seethed through me as I watched him. One feeling was partly admiration that he should be able to concentrate with such intensity that he didn't seem able to notice the danger he was in. The other feeling was one of the most bitter disgust as if I were watching a gaze that had gone beyond the human and which was as
15 indifferent to the outcome as a hawk's might be. You may think I was wrong in what I did next. I deliberately came up behind him and upset the chair so that he fell down head over heels in the middle of a brush-stroke. He turned on me such a gaze of blind fury that I was reminded of a rat which had once leapt at me from a river bank, and he would have struck me but that I pinioned his arms behind his back. I would have beaten him if his mother hadn't
20 come and taken him away, still snarling and weeping tears of rage. In spite of my almost religious fear at that moment, I tore the painting into small pieces and scattered them about the earth. Some people have since said that what I wanted to do was to protect the good name of the village but I must in all honesty say that that was not in my mind when I pushed the chair over. All that was in my mind was fury and disgust that this painter should have
25 watched this fight with such cold concentration that he seemed to think that the fight had been set up for him to paint, much as a house exists or an old wall.

It is true that after this no one would speak to our wonderful painter; we felt in him a presence more disturbing than Red Roderick who did after all recover. So disturbed were we by the incident that we would not even retain the happy paintings he had once
30 painted and which we had bought from him, those of the snow and the harvest, but tore them up and threw them on the dung heap.

MARKS

Questions

28. Look at lines 2–5 ("No, as I stood . . . bothered me").

    By referring to **one** example of the writer's use of language explain how William's reaction to the fight is made clear. **2**

29. Look at lines 6–8 ("As the scythes . . . snarl").

    With reference to **two** examples from these lines explain how the writer uses language to describe the dramatic nature of the fight. **4**

30. Look at lines 11–20 ("I cannot . . . tears of rage").

    Explain, in your own words as far as possible, why the narrator felt "admiration" and/or "bitter disgust" towards William the painter. You should make **four** key points in your answer. **4**

31. Look at lines 27–31.

    Explain, using your own words as far as possible, how the villagers react to William after the fight. You should make **two** key points in your answer. **2**

32. With reference to this extract, and to at least one other story by Iain Crichton Smith, show how the writer creates characters who do not appear to fit in with their surroundings. **8**

[Turn over

OR

Text 5 — Prose

If you choose this text you may not attempt a question on Prose in Section 2.

Read the extract below and then attempt the following questions.

***Dear Santa* by Anne Donovan**

Christmas Eve ah'm sittin on the bed in ma pyjamas wi a pad of blue lined paper and a Biro. The room is daurk but the wee bedside lamp makes a white circle that lights up the page ah'm starin at. It's hard tae find the words.

    Dear Santa,

5   *Please could you*

    I would like

    If its no too much bother

But what is it ah'm tryin tae say? Could you make ma mammy love me? That's no Santa's job, he's there tae gie oot sweeties and toys tae weans wanst a year, so there's nae point

10 in askin him. If there is a Santa. Ah look oot the windae; the sky's dirty grey and ah don't think we'll huv a white Christmas somehow.

The door opens and ma mammy comes in. The hall light's on and her fair hair sticks oot all roon her heid, fuzzy and soft. A cannae see her face.

    Are ye no asleep yet? It's nine o'clock.

15   *Ah'm writin ma letter tae Santa.*

    Santa doesnae come if yer no sleepin. Look, there's Katie, sound.

She bends ower Katie's bed, where she's lyin wi wan airm stickin oot fae under the covers. Ma mammy lifts the bedclothes ower her, then turns tae me.

    Hurry up and finish that letter, Alison. Ah'll pit it in fronty the fire and Santa'll get it

20 *when he comes.*

Ma mammy sits on the bed beside me while ah take a clean bit of paper and write dead slow so it's ma best writin.

    Dear Santa,

    Please could i have a Barbie doll, and a toy dog. I am a good girl.

25   *Love*

    Alison

Ah fold the paper twice, print SANTA on the front, then gie it tae ma mammy. She pits it in her pocket and lifts the covers fur me tae get inside. Ah coorie doon, watchin her hair glowin like a halo against the blackness of the room. Ah love strokin her hair, it's that soft

30 and fuzzy but she cannae be bothered wi that and jerks her heid away, sayin don't, you'll mess it up, just lik she does when ma daddy tries tae touch it. But it's that quiet and still and she's in a good mood so ah lift ma haun and touch her hair, just a wee bit.

MARKS

Mammy, how come you've got fair hair and Katie's got fair hair and mines is broon?

You take efter yer daddy and Katie takes efter me.

35 *Ah wisht ah had fair hair.*

How? There's nothing wrang wi broon hair.

Ah wisht ah had hair lik yours.

Ma mammy smiles and the lines roon her eyes get deeper but she looks at me mair soft like.

40 *Go tae sleep hen, or Santa'll no come.*

She bends ower and kisses me, a dry kiss, barely grazin ma cheek, and before ah have time tae kiss her back she's switched off the bedside light, stood up and moved tae the door.

Night, Alison.

Night, Mammy.

45 She goes oot, nearly closin the door, but leavin a wee crack of light fallin across the bedclothes.

Questions

33. Using your own words as far as possible, summarise what happens in the extract. You should make **four** key points.   4

34. With reference to lines 1-11, explain how **two** examples of Donovan's use of language help the reader to understand how Alison finds the task of writing the letter.   4

35. Look at lines 27-46.

   (a) Explain how **one** example of Donovan's language helps the reader understand there is a **positive** aspect to Alison's relationship with her mother.   2

   (b) Explain how **one** example of Donovan's language helps the reader understand there is a **negative** aspect to Alison's relationship with her mother.   2

36. Characters in Donovan's stories often face personal difficulties. With reference to the extract and to at least one other story, show how personal difficulties are explored.   8

[Turn over

SECTION 1 — SCOTTISH TEXT — 20 marks

PART C — SCOTTISH TEXT — POETRY

Text 1 — Poetry

If you choose this text you may not attempt a question on Poetry in Section 2.

Read the poem below and then attempt the following questions.

Originally by Carol Ann Duffy

We came from our own country in a red room
which fell through the fields, our mother singing
our father's name to the turn of the wheels.
My brothers cried, one of them bawling, *Home,*
5   *Home*, as the miles rushed back to the city,
the street, the house, the vacant rooms
where we didn't live any more. I stared
at the eyes of a blind toy, holding its paw.

All childhood is an emigration. Some are slow,
10   leaving you standing, resigned, up an avenue
where no one you know stays. Others are sudden.
Your accent wrong. Corners, which seem familiar,
leading to unimagined pebble-dashed estates, big boys
eating worms and shouting words you don't understand.
15   My parents' anxieties stirred like a loose tooth
in my head. *I want our own country*, I said.

But then you forget, or don't recall, or change,
and, seeing your brother swallow a slug, feel only
a skelf of shame. I remember my tongue
20   shedding its skin like a snake, my voice
in the classroom sounding just like the rest. Do I only think
I lost a river, culture, speech, sense of first space
and the right place? Now, *Where do you come from?*
strangers ask. *Originally?* And I hesitate.

MARKS

Questions

37. Look at lines 1-8.

Explain, using your own words as far as possible, what the poet/persona remembers about the journey. You should make **two** key points.

2

38. By referring to **two** examples of the poet's use of language in lines 9-16, explain fully how the poet makes clear the effect(s) of moving home.

4

39. Look at lines 17-21 ("But then . . . like the rest").

By referring to **two** examples of the poet's use of language explain fully how the poet suggests acceptance of the move.

4

40. Look at the last four words of the poem ("*Originally*? . . . hesitate").

Explain how any part of this makes an effective ending to the poem.

2

41. By referring closely to this poem, and to at least one other poem by Duffy, show how the poet uses word choice and/or imagery effectively to convey theme(s).

8

[Turn over

OR

Text 2 — Poetry

If you choose this text you may not attempt a question on Poetry in Section 2.

Read the poem below and then attempt the following questions.

Good Friday **by Edwin Morgan**

Three o'clock. The bus lurches
round into the sun. 'D's this go – '
he flops beside me – 'right along Bath Street?
– Oh tha's, tha's all right, see I've
5   got to get some Easter eggs for the kiddies.
I've had a wee drink, ye understand –
ye'll maybe think it's a – funny day
to be celebrating – well, no, but ye see
I wasny working, and I like to celebrate
10   when I'm no working – I don't say it's right
I'm no saying it's right, ye understand – ye understand?
But anyway tha's the way I look at it –
I'm no boring you, eh? – ye see today,
take today, I don't know what today's in aid of,
15   whether Christ was – crucified or was he –
rose fae the dead like, see what I mean?
You're an educatit man, you can tell me –
– Aye, well. There ye are. It's been seen
time and again, the working man
20   has nae education, he jist canny – jist
hasny got it, know what I mean,
he's jist bliddy ignorant – Christ aye,
bliddy ignorant. Well –' The bus brakes violently,
he lunges for the stair, swings down – off,
25   into the sun for his Easter eggs,
on very
            nearly
                    steady
                            legs.

Questions

42. Look at lines 2–13 ("D's this go . . . boring you, eh?").

    By referring to two examples of his speech, explain **two** things we learn about the drunk man.   **4**

43. Look at lines 14–23.

    (a) Comment on the effectiveness of **one** feature of the poet's use of language in creating realistic speech.   **2**

    (b) Show how any **two** examples of the use of word choice makes clear the poem's main ideas or central concerns.   **4**

44. How effective do you find lines 23–29 as a conclusion to the poem? You should refer to **one** example from these lines and to the ideas and/or language of the rest of the poem.   **2**

45. By referring closely to this poem and to at least one other poem, show how Morgan explores important human themes.   **8**

[Turn over

OR

Text 3 — Poetry

If you choose this text you may not attempt a question on Poetry in Section 2.

Read the poem below and then attempt the following questions.

***Sounds of the day* by Norman MacCaig**

When a clatter came,
it was horses crossing the ford.
When the air creaked, it was
a lapwing seeing us off the premises
5   of its private marsh. A snuffling puff
ten yards from the boat was the tide blocking and
unblocking a hole in a rock.
When the black drums rolled, it was water
falling sixty feet into itself.

10   When the door
scraped shut, it was the end
of all the sounds there are.

You left me
beside the quietest fire in the world.

15   I thought I was hurt in my pride only,
forgetting that,
when you plunge your hand in freezing water,
you feel
a bangle of ice round your wrist
20   before the whole hand goes numb.

Questions

MARKS

46. Look at lines 1-9.

Explain fully, in your own words as far as possible, how the poet feels about the "sounds of the day".

2

47. Look again at lines 1-9.

By referring to **one** example of the poet's word choice, explain how the poet suggests that disturbance or upset is to follow.

2

48. Look at lines 10-14.

By referring to **two** examples of the writer's use of language, explain fully how the poet makes it clear that the mood or atmosphere of the poem has now changed.

4

49. Look at lines 15-20.

By referring to **two** examples of word choice or imagery, explain fully how the poet makes clear the effects of his experience.

4

50. By referring to this poem, and to at least one other by MacCaig, show how strong feelings are a feature of his poetry.

8

[Turn over

OR

Text 4 — Poetry

If you choose this text you may not attempt a question on Poetry in Section 2.

Read the poem below and then attempt the following questions.

Keeping Orchids **by Jackie Kay**

The orchids my mother gave me when we first met
are still alive, twelve days later. Although

some of the buds remain closed as secrets.
Twice since I carried them back, like a baby in a shawl,

5   from her train station to mine, then home. Twice
since then the whole glass carafe has crashed

falling over, unprovoked, soaking my chest of drawers.
All the broken waters. I have rearranged

the upset orchids with troubled hands. Even after
10   that the closed ones did not open out. The skin

shut like an eye in the dark; the closed lid.
Twelve days later, my mother's hands are all I have.

Her face is fading fast. Even her voice rushes
through a tunnel the other way from home.

15   I close my eyes and try to remember exactly:
a paisley pattern scarf, a brooch, a navy coat.

A digital watch her daughter was wearing when she died.
Now they hang their heads,

and suddenly grow old — the proof of meeting. Still,
20   her hands, awkward and hard to hold

fold and unfold a green carrier bag as she tells
the story of her life. Compressed. Airtight.

A sad square, then a crumpled shape. A bag of tricks.
Her secret life — a hidden album, a box of love letters.

25   A door opens and closes. Time is outside waiting.
I catch the draught in my winter room.

Airlocks keep the cold air out.
Boiling water makes flowers live longer. So does

cutting the stems with a sharp knife.

Questions

MARKS

51. Using your own words as far as possible, explain what happens in lines 1-10 of this poem. You should make **two** key points.

2

52. Look again at lines 1-13 ("The orchids . . . fading fast.").

    Explain how the poet uses **one** example of word choice and **one** feature of structure to develop the idea of time.

4

53. Look at lines 13-29 ("Even her voice . . . sharp knife.").

    By referring to **three** examples of the poet's use of language, explain how the poet creates a sense of awkwardness about the meeting.

6

54. By referring closely to this poem and to at least one other poem by Kay, show how the poet uses personal experience to explore wider themes.

8

[END OF SECTION 1]

[Turn over

SECTION 2 — CRITICAL ESSAY — 20 marks

Attempt ONE question from the following genres — Drama, Prose, Poetry, Film and Television Drama, or Language.

Your answer must be on a different genre from that chosen in Section 1.

You should spend approximately 45 minutes on this Section.

DRAMA

> *Answers to questions in this part should refer to the text and to such relevant features as characterisation, key scene(s), structure, climax, theme, plot, conflict, setting . . .*

1. Choose a play which explores an important relationship, for example, husband and wife, leader and follower, parent and child, or any other relationship.

    Describe this relationship and then, by referring to appropriate techniques, explain how the relationship develops.

2. Choose a play which explores an issue or theme which interests you.

    By referring to appropriate techniques, explain how this issue or theme is explored.

PROSE

> *Answers to questions in this part should refer to the text and to such relevant features as characterisation, setting, language, key incident(s), climax, turning point, plot, structure, narrative technique, theme, ideas, description . . .*

3. Choose a novel **or** short story **or** work of non-fiction which has a key moment.

    Give a brief account of the key moment and, by referring to appropriate techniques, show how it is significant to the text as a whole.

4. Choose a novel **or** short story in which there is an interesting character.

    By referring to appropriate techniques, show how the author makes the character interesting.

POETRY

> *Answers to questions in this part should refer to the text and to such relevant features as word choice, tone, imagery, structure, content, rhythm, rhyme, theme, sound, ideas . . .*

5. Choose a poem which describes a person or a place or an event in a memorable way.

   By referring to poetic techniques, explain how the poet makes this poem so memorable.

6. Choose a poem which deals with a powerful emotion.

   By referring to poetic techniques, show how the poet creates the powerful emotion.

FILM AND TELEVISION DRAMA

> *Answers to questions in this part should refer to the text and to such relevant features as use of camera, key sequence, characterisation, mise-en-scène, editing, setting, music/sound, special effects, plot, dialogue . . .*

7. Choose a scene or sequence from a film or TV drama which shocks or surprises you in some way.

   By referring to appropriate techniques, show how in this scene or sequence the element of surprise is made effective.

8. Choose a film or TV drama in which there is a character about whom you have mixed feelings.

   Show why this character is important to the film or TV drama as a whole and by referring to appropriate techniques, explain how these mixed feelings are created.

* "TV drama" includes a single play, a series or a serial.

[Turn over

LANGUAGE

Answers to questions in this part should refer to the text and to such relevant features as register, accent, dialect, slang, jargon, vocabulary, tone, abbreviation . . .

9. Choose an advertisement which aims to persuade you to buy a product, or to support the aims of a particular group.

    By referring to specific examples from the advertisement, explain how persuasive language is used.

10. Consider the distinctive language used by any group of people from the same place, or with the same job, or the same interest . . .

    By referring to specific examples, explain how the distinctive language of the group is different from the language used by the general population.

[END OF SECTION 2]

[END OF QUESTION PAPER]

NATIONAL 5

2017

National Qualifications 2017

X724/75/11

**English
Reading for Understanding,
Analysis and Evaluation**

FRIDAY, 12 MAY

9:00 AM – 10:00 AM

Total marks — 30

Attempt ALL questions.

Write your answers clearly in the answer booklet provided. In the answer booklet you must clearly identify the question number you are attempting.

Use **blue** or **black** ink.

Before leaving the examination room you must give your answer booklet to the Invigilator; if you do not, you may lose all the marks for this paper.

Resilience

My best friend, Mark, was a keen footballer. We played in my back garden every afternoon as kids, often down the local park, sometimes other kids would join us, and in the summer we never seemed to leave.

I often think of those long, endlessly absorbing days, game after game, sometimes until it got dark
5 and we played by the dim glow of street lights. In the summer holidays, my mum would make a two-litre bottle of orange squash and we would pass it from player to player at half-time, none of us deterred by the fact it had got warm in the sun. My, it tasted good.

Mark never made it into the school team. He kept trying, kept going to the "trials", both at primary and senior school, but he was just off the pace. The disappointment was always bitter.
10 You could see it on his face. He yearned to play, to progress, to be able to read out a match report at school assembly (one of the honours of making the team). But he never did.

It has been reported that 98 per cent of those signed by English teams at 16 fail to make the transition into professional football. Many struggle to cope with rejection at such a tender age. Clinical psychologists report that many suffer anxiety, a loss of confidence and, in some cases,
15 depression. These youngsters are often described as being "left on football's scrapheap".

It seems to me, though, that the number rejected is, in fact, far higher. After all, the sifting process starts from the first time you kick a ball at the local park. I was one of the few who made it into my school team (I captained it). But when I went to trial for the district team, surrounded by the best players from all the schools in the area, the standard was high. Parents were
20 everywhere. I remember my heart beating out of my chest when the "scouts" arrived. I did not make it. I was crushed by the disappointment. How could it be otherwise? But I also realised that the race had only just started for those who had made the cut. Of those who made it into the district team, only a handful were picked by Reading, the local club. And of those who made it to Reading, only a fraction made it into professional football. Perhaps none made it all the way to
25 the top flight.

And that really is the point. When we watch any Premier League match, we are witnessing players who have made it through a filtering process of staggering dimensions. It is a process that does not merely discard 98 per cent of those who aspire, but something closer to 99·9999 per cent. For every first-team player, there are millions of others, like grains of sand on the beach, who have
30 tried, who have dreamt, but who have failed.

The majority, like Mark, never made it through the first lap. Others made it to the final straight, before dropping out. But this is football. This is life. Failure is an inevitable aspect of any competition worthy of the name. Without losers, there cannot be winners. Without pain, there cannot be joy. Without natural selection, there cannot be evolution. Failure is not the opposite of
35 progress; failure is part and parcel of progress.

Take a step back and you will see that football is a beautiful meritocracy. That so many dreams are shattered is testament to just how many dared to dream in the first place. The skills are transparent, the opportunities exist. There is no room for family favours or cosy alliances. The best of the best shine through, whether they are from a tough part of Liverpool, like Wayne
40 Rooney, or raised in grinding poverty in Uruguay, like Luis Suárez.

And the important point is that clubs have a responsibility to those who make it as far as the academies. They have a responsibility to create rounded people, with decent educations. Parents must support this approach, too, rather than exerting undue pressure on often vulnerable children. This is not just about giving youngsters a plan B; it is also about enlightened
45 self-interest.

Youngsters who are educated and self-assured are likely to be better footballers, too. The Ancient Greeks understood this only too well. They created strong links between the gymnasiums and the academies and embraced the humane idea that the mind and body grow together. The German football system has embraced this truth, too. The clubs there want intelligent and confident
50 young men. Such a cultural transformation needs to happen here, too. But I wish to make a deeper point. It is that we need to redefine our relationship with failure, not just in football but in life. We need to remind our children that losing is an essential (indeed, a beautiful) part of life. We need to emphasise the empowering idea that failure is less important, infinitely less so, than how we respond to it. Failing to make the grade at football is crushing. It is natural to be sad. But
55 it is also a pathway to a new reality.

Tens of thousands do not make it to Oxford or Cambridge. Hundreds of thousands of actors never win an Oscar. Tens of millions fail to make it into Manchester United or Chelsea. But this is not the end of life. It is merely the beginning. It is an opportunity to conceive a new dream, a new hope, a new way of finding meaning in this curious journey called life.

60 I often think about Mark. And I am thankful that his failures in football, so important, so trivial, never deterred him. He created new dreams, new aspirations, and lived a life that inspired all who knew him.

Life is too short, too precious, to be derailed by failure. We have to accept it. We have to embrace it.

Matthew Syed, in "The Times"

MARKS

Total marks — 30
Attempt ALL Questions

1. Look at lines 1—7, and explain how **one** example of the writer's word choice makes it clear that his memories of childhood football are positive.

    2

2. Look at lines 8—11, and explain **in your own words** why Mark was so disappointed.

    You should make **four** key points in your answer.

    4

3. Look at lines 12—25, and identify **in your own words six** points which the writer makes about young people hoping to become professional footballers.

    6

4. Explain fully why the simile "like grains of sand on the beach" (line 29) is effective here.

    2

5. Look at lines 31—35. By referring to **two** language features, explain how the writer makes clear his view about competition.

    You should refer to **two different** features such as word choice, imagery or sentence structure.

    4

6. The writer tells us that "football is a beautiful meritocracy" (line 36).

    Explain **in your own words three** points the writer makes about merit being rewarded in the rest of this paragraph.

    3

7. Look at lines 46—55, and identify, **in your own words** as far as possible, **five** points the writer makes in these lines about sport and/or life.

    5

8. Look at lines 56—59, and explain how **one** feature of the writer's sentence structure is used to highlight an important point.

    2

9. Select any expression in lines 60—64, and explain how it contributes to the passage's effective conclusion.

    2

[END OF QUESTION PAPER]

OPEN OUT FOR QUESTIONS

DO NOT WRITE ON THIS PAGE

[BLANK PAGE]

DO NOT WRITE ON THIS PAGE

National Qualifications 2017

X724/75/12

English
Critical Reading

FRIDAY, 12 MAY

10:20 AM – 11:50 AM

Total marks — 40

SECTION 1 — Scottish Text — 20 marks

Read an extract from a Scottish text you have previously studied.

Choose ONE text from either

Part A — Drama   Pages 2—7

or

Part B — Prose   Pages 8—17

or

Part C — Poetry   Pages 18—25

Attempt ALL the questions for your chosen text.

SECTION 2 — Critical Essay — 20 marks

Attempt ONE question from the following genres — Drama, Prose, Poetry, Film and Television Drama, or Language.

Your answer must be on a different genre from that chosen in Section 1.

You should spend approximately 45 minutes on each Section.

Write your answers clearly in the answer booklet provided. In the answer booklet you must clearly identify the question number you are attempting.

Use **blue** or **black** ink.

Before leaving the examination room you must give your answer booklet to the Invigilator; if you do not, you may lose all the marks for this paper.

SECTION 1 — SCOTTISH TEXT — 20 marks

PART A — SCOTTISH TEXT — DRAMA

Text 1 — Drama

If you choose this text you may not attempt a question on Drama in Section 2.

Read the extract below and then attempt the following questions.

Bold Girls **by Rona Munro**

Extract from Scene Two (The women are in a social club . . .)

	CASSIE:	It's the D.T.s.
	NORA:	It's the R.U.C.
	CASSIE:	Oh don't let it get to you.
	NORA:	So let's see your hand!
5		*Cassie holds hers out, it is also shaking*
	CASSIE:	It's our life style Mummy, we'll have to change our life style.
	NORA:	Is that right?
	CASSIE:	We're living too fast so we are, it's the same problem the film stars have, we'll burn ourselves out with all the excitement.
10	NORA:	Me and Joan Collins both.
	CASSIE:	You can write articles for the women's magazines, "Stop and Search, would your manicure stand up to the closest inspection?"
	NORA:	Let's see Marie's hand there.
		Marie is lost in her own thoughts
15		*Cassie pulls Marie's hand out, Nora and Cassie study it*
	CASSIE:	Steady as a rock.
	NORA:	Ah she's got a clear conscience.
	CASSIE:	Either that or she's in a coma, are you with us, Marie?
	MARIE:	Hmmm?
20	NORA:	Wired up but not plugged in.
	MARIE:	Are you reading my palm?
	CASSIE:	I will if you like.
		Deirdre approaches their table with a tray of drinks
		Cassie glances up at her, then bends theatrically over Marie's hand
25	CASSIE:	Oh, you're going to meet a dark stranger Marie, all in white but with a black wee heart. You better watch out for she'll thieve the clothes off your back but you'll not have peace till you nail the wee snake down and ask her what she's up to.

MARKS

30 DEIRDRE: (*handing out the drinks correctly*) Black Russian — gin and lime — Pernod and blackcurrant.

CASSIE: So what about you Deirdre, if it is Deirdre?

DEIRDRE: It is.

MARIE: Cassie . . .

35 CASSIE: I hope you've not taken a fancy to anything else that's caught your eye, like my handbag.

DEIRDRE: (*staring at Cassie for a minute*) It was in a car. A blue car.

CASSIE: What?

DEIRDRE: That I saw you before.

CASSIE: You're a lying hoor, you never saw anything.

40 DEIRDRE: With a man. With him. With —

Cassie lunges at her before she can get another word out

Questions

1. Using your own words as far as possible, identify **four** things you learn about the women's lives in this extract.   4

2. Look at lines 1—12.

    Identify **one** example of humour and explain why it is effective.   2

3. Look at lines 13—35.

    (a) By referring to **one** example of word choice, explain how the playwright reveals the relationship between Nora and Marie.   2

    (b) By referring to **one** example of word choice, explain how the playwright reveals the relationship between Cassie and Deirdre.   2

4. Look at lines 36—41.

    By referring to **one** example of the writer's use of language, explain how this extract ends with a moment of tension.   2

5. By referring to this extract and to elsewhere in the play, show how mother and daughter-type relationships are explored.   8

[Turn over

OR

Text 2 — Drama

If you choose this text you may not attempt a question on Drama in Section 2.

Read the extract below and then attempt the following questions.

Sailmaker by Alan Spence

ALEC: What is it that gets intae ye? Wi the bettin ah mean?

DAVIE: Ah don't know. Just wan a these things.

        Ah suppose it's the feelin you've at least got a *chance*.

        Is there any wood in there? The paper just flares up then dies.

5   (*ALEC empties out contents of box, hands box to DAVIE*)

DAVIE: Great. (*Starts breaking up box, ALEC goes out, comes back with canvas tool-bag, cane bow. Fires imaginary arrow*) Bring me my bow of burning gold, eh?

        (*ALEC breaks bow for fire*)

        That's more like it. (*Warms himself*)

10   That's the stuff.

ALEC: (*Taking tools from canvas bag*) Look at this.

DAVIE: God. Ma auld sailmakin tools. (*Takes wooden marlinspike*) Ah was an apprentice when ah was your age. Hard work it wis tae.

        Ah worked on the Queen Mary ye know.

15 ALEC: Aye.

DAVIE: Worked on destroyers durin the War. Made gun-covers, awnings, tarpaulins.

        Made this wee bag!

ALEC: Did ye?

DAVIE: Oh aye. Used tae make leather wallets an things.

20   Made a shopping bag for yer mother. Made you a swing! Wi a big sorta bucket seat. Used tae hang it in the doorway there.

ALEC: Ah remember!

        You could still be makin things. Sellin them.

        (*DAVIE nods, shrugs*)

25   Could ye no go back tae yer trade?

DAVIE: Nae demand. Was different durin the War. They needed us then awright. Reserved occupation it was. Meant ah couldnae sign up. Been goin downhill since then but. Yards shuttin doon. Look at Harland's. Or where it was. Just a big empty space covered wi weeds.

30   Yer Uncle Billy had the right idea. Took his redundancy money and moved tae Aberdeen. Doin all right.

ALEC: Ian's an Aberdeen supporter now.

MARKS

DAVIE: Billy'll disown him for that!

ALEC: Did you ever think about movin?

35 DAVIE: Thought about it. (*Shrugs*) Thing is Billy bein a painter had more chance ae a job. Ah backed a loser right fae the start. Then it got even worse. They started bringin in aw the manmade fibres, usin machines. Got lassies daein hauf the work. Dead loss.

So for God's sake you dae somethin wi *your* life!

Questions

6. By referring to **two** examples from anywhere in this extract, explain how Alec's attitude towards Davie is revealed at this point in the play.   4

7. Look at lines 14—21.

By referring to **two** examples of language, explain how the writer suggests Davie's enthusiasm for his old trade.   4

8. Look at lines 26—38.

By referring to **two** examples of language, explain how the writer makes it clear that Davie's old trade is not important any more.   4

9. By referring to this extract and to elsewhere in the play, show how the character of Davie is presented.   8

[Turn over

OR

Text 3 — Drama

If you choose this text you may not attempt a question on Drama in Section 2.

Read the extract below and then attempt the following questions.

Tally's Blood by Ann Marie Di Mambro

ROSINELLA:	You don't see it, do you? It's up to me to see everything.
MASSIMO:	See what?
ROSINELLA:	Why do you think she was in that state, eh?
MASSIMO:	Over the wedding.
5 ROSINELLA:	Stupid eejit. Over Hughie, you mean.
MASSIMO:	Hughie?
ROSINELLA:	You no see the way he looks at our Lucia? He's crazy for her.
MASSIMO:	Away you go. They grew up together.
ROSINELLA:	She's to marry an Italian.
10 MASSIMO:	For God's sake, Rosie, she's no asking to marry him, just to go to his brother's wedding. You worry too much.
ROSINELLA:	No, Massimo. I don't worry enough. It's been going on before my eyes and I've never seen it till tonight.
MASSIMO:	Seen what?
15 ROSINELLA:	It's bad enough he's fell for her. But don't tell me she's to get falling for him. I'll soon put a stop to this before it starts.
MASSIMO:	(*Groans*) Rosie . . .
ROSINELLA:	Italians are not interested in a lassie that's been out with anybody else — especially the Scotch men. They like a girl that's kept herself for them. I'm surprised at you.
20	
MASSIMO:	What have I done now?
ROSINELLA:	Are you forgetting what this country did to the Italians during the war? (*Massimo groans*) They took you out of here as if you were a thief.
MASSIMO:	Listen, Rosie, all I care about the war is that it's over. I lost ma faither, ma brother and four years out ma life.
25	
ROSINELLA:	Well, I'll never get over it.
MASSIMO:	Neither will I. But everybody suffered. Not just us.
ROSINELLA:	Italians have got to stick together.
MASSIMO:	Then come to Italy with me, Rosie, what do you say?
30	*Rosinella uncomfortable at mention of Italy.*
ROSINELLA:	No . . . I don't think so.
MASSIMO:	A wee holiday. The three of us.

ROSINELLA: Not yet, Massimo. You go, yourself. I don't mind.

35   MASSIMO: Everybody was asking for you when I was over. Asking why you've never been back. Please, Rosie, I'm dying to show you my daddy's house. You can help me make it nice. Next year, maybe, eh? How about it, Rosie?

ROSINELLA: I'm not going anywhere, Massimo, not until I see Lucia settled. (*A beat*) You think she's calmed down now? I think I'll take her to Glasgow on Saturday, go round the shops, get her something nice, take her to Palombo's to get her
40   hair done. I'll go and tell her.

Questions

10.   Look at lines 1—17.

Using your own words as far as possible, identify the key areas of disagreement between Rosinella and Massimo. You should make **four** key points in your answer.   4

11.   Look at lines 9—20.

By referring to **two** examples of language, explain what is revealed about Rosinella's character.   4

12.   Look at lines 22—27.

By referring to **two** examples from their dialogue, explain how Rosinella and Massimo's different attitudes to the war are revealed.   4

13.   By referring to this extract and to elsewhere in the play, show how the character of Massimo is presented.   8

[Turn over

SECTION 1 — SCOTTISH TEXT — 20 marks

PART B — SCOTTISH TEXT — PROSE

Text 1 — Prose

If you choose this text you may not attempt a question on Prose in Section 2.

Read the extract below and then attempt the following questions.

***The Cone-Gatherers* by Robin Jenkins**

In this extract from Chapter One, Duror is watching the cone-gatherers' hut.

The hut was lit by oil-lamp. He smelled paraffin as well as woodsmoke. He knew they picked up old cones to kindle the fire, and on Sunday they had worked for hours sawing up blown timber for firewood: they had been given permission to do so. The only window was not in the wall facing him, so that he could not see inside; but he had been in their hut so
5 often, they were in his imagination so vividly, and he was so close every sound they made could be interpreted; therefore it was easy for him to picture them as they went about making their meal. They peeled their potatoes the night before, and left them in a pot of cold water. They did not wash before they started to cook or eat. They did not change their clothes. They had no table; an upturned box did instead, with a newspaper for a
10 cloth; and each sat on his own bed. They seldom spoke. All evening they would be dumb, the taller brooding over a days-old paper, the dwarf carving some animal out of wood: at present he was making a squirrel. Seeing it half-finished that afternoon, holding it shudderingly in his hands, Duror had against his will, against indeed the whole frenzied thrust of his being, sensed the kinship between the carver and the creature whose likeness
15 he was carving. When complete, the squirrel would be not only recognisable, it would be almost alive. To Duror it had been the final defeat that such ability should be in a half-man, a freak, an imbecile. He had read that the Germans were putting idiots and cripples to death in gas chambers. Outwardly, as everybody expected, he condemned such barbarity; inwardly, thinking of idiocy and crippledness not as abstractions but as
20 embodied in the crouch-backed cone-gatherer, he had profoundly approved.

At last he roused himself and moved away. Yet, though he was going home, he felt he was leaving behind him in that hut something unresolved, which would never cease to torment him. It was almost as if there were not two brothers, but three; he himself was the third. Once he halted and looked back. His fists tightened on his gun. He saw himself returning,
25 kicking open the door, shouting at them his disgust, and then blasting them both to everlasting perdition. He felt an icy hand on his brow as he imagined that hideous but liberating fratricide.

Questions

14. Look at lines 1—12.

Using your own words as far as possible, identify **four** things we learn about how the cone-gatherers live.

4

15. Look at lines 12—20.

By referring to **two** examples of language, explain how the writer makes clear Duror's feelings towards the cone-gatherers.

4

16. Look at lines 21—27.

By referring to **two** examples of language, explain how Duror feels at this point.

4

17. By referring to this extract and to elsewhere in the novel, show how the theme of good versus evil is explored.

8

[Turn over

OR

Text 2 — Prose

If you choose this text you may not attempt a question on Prose in Section 2.

Read the extract below and then attempt the following questions.

***The Testament of Gideon Mack* by James Robertson**

This extract is taken from the section of the novel where Gideon is relating his experience in the cave with the Devil after falling into the Black Jaws.

"You must understand," I said, "that I've never seriously thought you existed at all. It's a bit of a shock now, to find you just a few miles from Monimaskit."

"Don't think you're privileged," he said, sparking up a bit. "Don't think I'm paying you some kind of special attention. I do like Scotland, though, I spend a lot of time here. I once
5   preached to some women at North Berwick who thought they were witches. They were burnt for it, poor cows. I preached at Auchtermuchty another time, disguised as one of your lot, a minister, but the folk there found me out. Fifers, thrawn buggers, they were too sharp. But I do like Scotland. I like the miserable weather. I like the miserable people, the fatalism, the negativity, the violence that's always just below the surface. And I like the way
10   you deal with religion. One century you're up to your lugs in it, the next you're trading the whole apparatus in for Sunday superstores. Praise the Lord and thrash the bairns. Ask and ye shall have the door shut in your face. Blessed are they that shop on the Sabbath, for they shall get the best bargains. Oh, yes, this is a very fine country."

In spite of his claimed affection for Scotland, he seemed morose and fed up. Suddenly he
15   brightened.

"I know what I'll do if you want proof. I'll do what I said I would. I'll fix your leg."

This did not strike me as a good idea. "No," I said. "A surgeon should do that."

"Please," he said. "I'd like to."

When I said no again I heard a low rumble growl round the cave, which I took to be the
20   precursor of another stupendous roar. I made no further protest. He went over to the fire and I saw him put his right hand into the flames, deep into the middle of them. He was elbow-deep in fire but he didn't even flinch. His jacket didn't catch alight, and his hand and arm were quite unaffected by the heat. He stayed like that for fully three minutes. Then he turned and his whole arm was a white, pulsating glow. He came towards me and
25   reached for my leg with that terrible arm, and I shrank away from him.

"It doesn't hurt me," he said, "and it won't hurt you. Don't move."

I was too terrified to move. I was still clutching my mug of tea and he took it from me with his left hand and placed it on the ground. I closed my eyes and waited for the burning agony, but it did not come. I was aware only of a slight tingling sensation on my right thigh.
30   I opened my eyes and looked down. There was intense concentration on his face. His hand was *inside* my leg. Where the bone bulged out the skin was sizzling and popping like bacon in a pan, but there was no pain, only this faint tickle. He was pushing and prodding the bone back into place, welding it together. Smoke and steam issued from my leg, but still there was no pain. I felt only an incredible warmth, like the warmth of the spirit in his
35   black bottle, spreading through my whole body. His hand twisted something and my leg gave an involuntary jolt. "Don't move," he snapped. "I couldn't help it," I said.

MARKS

Questions

18. Look at lines 3—18.

    Using your own words as far as possible, identify **three** things we learn about the Devil.   **3**

19. Look at lines 19—36.

    By referring to **one** example, explain how language is used to show Gideon's fear.   **2**

20. Look again at lines 19—36.

    Using your own words as far as possible, explain how the Devil fixes Gideon's leg. You should make **three** key points in your answer.   **3**

21. In this extract the devil's mood changes. By referring to **two** examples of language from anywhere in the extract, explain how the writer makes this clear.   **4**

22. By referring to this extract and to elsewhere in the novel, show how meeting the Devil affects the character of Gideon Mack.   **8**

[Turn over

OR

Text 3 — Prose

If you choose this text you may not attempt a question on Prose in Section 2.

Read the extract below and then attempt the following questions.

Kidnapped **by Robert Louis Stevenson**

In this extract from Chapter 20, David Balfour and Alan Breck Stewart are on the run after the killing of Red Fox.

The first peep of morning, then, showed us this horrible place, and I could see Alan knit his brow.

"This is no fit place for you and me," he said. "This is a place they're bound to watch."

And with that he ran harder than ever down to the water side, in a part where the river
5   was split in two among three rocks. It went through with a horrid thundering that made my belly quake; and there hung over the lynn a little mist of spray. Alan looked neither to the right nor to the left, but jumped clean upon the middle rock and fell there on his hands and knees to check himself, for that rock was small and he might have pitched over on the far side. I had scarce time to measure the distance or to understand the peril before I had
10   followed him, and he had caught and stopped me.

So there we stood, side by side upon a small rock slippery with spray, a far broader leap in front of us, and the river dinning upon all sides. When I saw where I was, there came on me a deadly sickness of fear, and I put my hand over my eyes. Alan took me and shook me; I saw he was speaking, but the roaring of the falls and the trouble of my mind prevented me
15   from hearing; only I saw his face was red with anger, and that he stamped upon the rock. The same look showed me the water raging by, and the mist hanging in the air: and with that I covered my eyes again and shuddered.

The next minute Alan had set the brandy bottle to my lips, and forced me to drink about a gill, which sent the blood into my head again. Then, putting his hands to his mouth and his
20   mouth to my ear, he shouted, "Hang or drown!" and turning his back upon me, leaped over the farther branch of the stream, and landed safe.

I was now alone upon the rock, which gave me the more room; the brandy was singing in my ears; I had this good example fresh before me, and just wit enough to see that if I did not leap at once, I should never leap at all. I bent low on my knees and flung myself forth,
25   with that kind of anger of despair that has sometimes stood me in stead of courage. Sure enough, it was but my hands that reached the full length; these slipped, caught again, slipped again; and I was sliddering back into the lynn, when Alan seized me, first by the hair, then by the collar, and with a great strain dragged me into safety.

Never a word he said, but set off running again for his life, and I must stagger to my feet
30   and run after him. I had been weary before, but now I was sick and bruised, and partly drunken with the brandy; I kept stumbling as I ran, I had a stitch that came near to overmaster me; and when at last Alan paused under a great rock that stood there among a number of others, it was none too soon for David Balfour.

MARKS

Questions

23. Using your own words as far as possible, summarise the main events in this extract. You should make **four** key points in your answer.   4

24. Look at lines 1—10.

    (a) Explain how **one** example of the writer's language shows that Alan is confident at this point in the extract.   2

    (b) Explain how **one** example of the writer's language shows how David feels at this point in the extract.   2

25. Look at lines 22—28.

    Explain how **one** example of sentence structure and **one** example of word choice contribute to the creation of drama at this point in the extract.   4

26. By referring to this extract and to elsewhere in the novel, show the ways in which Alan supports David physically **and/or** emotionally throughout the novel.   8

[Turn over

OR

Text 4 — Prose

If you choose this text you may not attempt a question on Prose in Section 2.

Read the extract below and then attempt the following questions.

The Crater by Iain Crichton Smith

On his hands and knees he squirmed forward, the others behind him. This was his first raid and he thought, "I am frightened." But it was different from being out in the open on a battlefield. It was an older fear, the fear of being buried in the earth, the fear of wandering through eternal passageways and meeting grey figures like weasels and fighting
5 with them in the darkness. He tested the wire. Thank God it had been cut. And then he thought, "Will we need the ladders?" The sides of the trenches were so deep sometimes that ladders were necessary to get out again. And as he crawled towards the German trenches he had a vision of Germans crawling beneath British trenches undermining them. A transparent imagined web hung below him in the darkness quivering with grey spiders.

10 He looked at his illuminated watch. The time was right. Then they were in the German trenches. The rest was a series of thrustings and flashes. Once he thought he saw or imagined he saw from outside a dugout a man sitting inside reading a book. It was like looking through a train window into a house before the house disappears. There were Mills bombs, hackings of bayonets, scurryings and breathings as of rats. A white face towered
15 above him, his pistol exploded and the face disappeared. There was a terrible stink all around him, and the flowing of blood. Then there was a long silence. Back. They must get back. He passed the order along. And then they wriggled back again avoiding the craters which lay around them, created by shells, and which were full of slimy water. If they fell into one of these they would be drowned. As he looked, shells began to fall into them
20 sending up huge spouts of water. Over the parapet. They were over the parapet. Crouched they had run and scrambled and were over. Two of them were carrying a third. They stumbled down the trench. There were more wounded than he had thought. Wright . . . one arm seemed to have been shot off. Sergeant Smith was bending over him. "You'll get sent home all right," he was saying. Some of the men were tugging at their equipment and
25 talking feverishly. Young Ellis was lying down, blood pouring from his mouth. Harris said, "Morrison's in the crater."

He and Sergeant Smith looked at each other. They were both thinking the same: there is no point, he's had it. They could see each other's eyes glaring whitely through the black, but could not tell the expression on the faces. The shells were still falling, drumming and
30 shaking the earth. All these craters out there, these dead moons.

Questions

27. Look at lines 1—9.

     By referring to **two** examples, explain how the writer's use of language makes clear the soldier's fear.

     4

28. Look at lines 11—16 ("The rest . . . flowing of blood").

     Using your own words as far as possible, identify **four** ways in which the trenches are horrific.

     4

29. Look at lines 16—21 ("Back . . . and were over").

     By referring to **one** example, explain how the sentence structure highlights the danger faced by the men.

     2

30. Look at lines 27—30.

     By referring to **one** example, explain how the writer's use of language creates a sense of despair.

     2

31. By referring to this extract and to at least one other story by Crichton Smith, show how he uses word choice **and/or** symbolism to highlight an important message.

     8

[Turn over

OR

Text 5 — Prose

If you choose this text you may not attempt a question on Prose in Section 2.

Read the extract below and then attempt the following questions.

Zimmerobics by Anne Donovan

So that was that. At 11am I assembled with the others in the dayroom. I knew most of their faces, but was surprised to see some of them wearing tracksuits and trainers. It hadn't occurred to me to ask what to wear and I didn't possess such things anyway, but somehow I felt out of place. It was like starting school and discovering that the others were wearing
5   school uniform and you weren't.

Cheryl bounced into the room, wearing a pair of trainers that made her feet look like a horse's hooves. Her hair was tied back with an emerald green band which matched her shimmering leotard and tights.

"I hope she doesn't need to go to the toilet in a hurry," muttered a voice behind me.

10 "Hi there. It's great to see so many of you here this morning. Now, take it at your own pace and if you feel uncomfortable or out of breath any time, stop for a wee rest. Enjoy!"

She switched on the music. We stood behind our Zimmers as she got us to stretch first one, then the other, arm, move our heads to each side, then stretch our legs. I heard a few creaking sounds but so far so good. We moved on to circling movements and, as the record
15 progressed, I felt an unaccustomed but pleasant tingling in my limbs.

"That was the warm-up. The next one's a bit faster."

The next record was a catchy tune about living in the YMCA. I couldn't keep up with the routine at first but, once we'd been through it a few times, I became quite proficient. We had to raise our right then our left arms to the Y and the M, then pause on the C and hold
20 our Zimmers as we bent both legs for the A. Then we marched (well, shuffled in most cases) round to the left, raised our left arms twice to the Y and the M (that was a bit tricky), paused at the C and kicked our left leg out to the A. During the verse we did some marching and a few kicks, then we repeated the chorus routine, this time moving to the right. At the end we clapped three times, boldly taking both hands off our Zimmer frames.

25 It was brilliant. I hadn't felt like this for years. My body was old and decrepit, but it still worked. I had been concentrating so hard on what I was doing I had forgotten the others, but now I looked round and saw their faces, flushed and smiling.

"You all did great. Give yourselves a round of applause." She clapped her hands above her head while we patted our hands together, slightly embarrassed.

30 "Same time next week," she called as we hirpled out of the dayroom, old once again.

The memory of the exercise class lingered on for the rest of the day, not just in my mind as I relived the routine, but in my bones and muscles. I thought I'd be sore and stiff but, surprisingly, I felt better, as though someone had oiled all the creaky old joints. There was a feeling in them which I suppose you would call an ache, but it was a pleasant ache, an
35 ache of life.

MARKS

Questions

32. Using your own words as far as possible, explain how Miss Knight's attitude to Zimmerobics changes over the extract. You should make **two** key points in your answer.

    2

33. Look at lines 12—35.

    By referring to **one** example, explain how the writer's use of language makes clear the problems associated with old age.

    2

34. Look again at lines 12—35.

    By referring to **two** examples, explain how the writer's use of language makes clear Miss Knight's feelings about exercise.

    4

35. Look at the extract as a whole.

    By referring to **two** examples, explain how the writer's use of language creates humour.

    4

36. By referring to this extract and to at least one other story, show how Donovan creates convincing characters.

    8

[Turn over

SECTION 1 — SCOTTISH TEXT — 20 marks

PART C — SCOTTISH TEXT — POETRY

Text 1 — Poetry

If you choose this text you may not attempt a question on Poetry in Section 2.

Read the poem below and then attempt the following questions.

War Photographer by Carol Ann Duffy

In his darkroom he is finally alone
with spools of suffering set out in ordered rows.
The only light is red and softly glows,
as though this were a church and he
5   a priest preparing to intone a Mass.
Belfast. Beirut. Phnom Penh. All flesh is grass.

He has a job to do. Solutions slop in trays
beneath his hands, which did not tremble then
though seem to now. Rural England. Home again
10 to ordinary pain which simple weather can dispel,
to fields which don't explode beneath the feet
of running children in a nightmare heat.

Something is happening. A stranger's features
faintly start to twist before his eyes,
15 a half-formed ghost. He remembers the cries
of this man's wife, how he sought approval
without words to do what someone must
and how the blood stained into foreign dust.

A hundred agonies in black and white
20 from which his editor will pick out five or six
for Sunday's supplement. The reader's eyeballs prick
with tears between the bath and pre-lunch beers.
From the aeroplane he stares impassively at where
he earns his living and they do not care.

Questions

MARKS

37. Look at lines 1—6.

By referring to **one** example of word choice, explain how the poet suggests that the war photographer is like "a priest" in "church".

2

38. Look at lines 9—12.

By referring to **two** examples of language, explain how the poet makes it clear that the war photographer's home country is very different from the countries he visits.

4

39. Look at lines 13—18.

By referring to **two** examples of language, explain how the poet makes it clear that the war photographer has been strongly affected by his experiences.

4

40. Look at lines 19—24.

Using your own words as far as possible, explain **two** key ideas explored in the final stanza.

2

41. By referring to this poem and to at least one other by Duffy, show how the idea of people suffering painful experiences is a feature of her poetry.

8

[Turn over

OR

Text 2 — Poetry

If you choose this text you may not attempt a question on Poetry in Section 2.

Read the poem below and then attempt the following questions.

Trio **by Edwin Morgan**

Coming up Buchanan Street, quickly, on a sharp winter evening
a young man and two girls, under the Christmas lights —
The young man carries a new guitar in his arms,
the girl on the inside carries a very young baby,
5   and the girl on the outside carries a chihuahua.
And the three of them are laughing, their breath rises
in a cloud of happiness, and as they pass
the boy says, 'Wait till he sees this but!'
The chihuahua has a tiny Royal Stewart tartan coat like a teapot-
10   holder,
the baby in its white shawl is all bright eyes and mouth like favours
        in a fresh sweet cake,
the guitar swells out under its milky plastic cover, tied at the neck
        with silver tinsel tape and a brisk sprig of mistletoe.
15   Orphean sprig! Melting baby! Warm chihuahua!
The vale of tears is powerless before you.
Whether Christ is born, or is not born, you
put paid to fate, it abdicates
                                under the Christmas lights.
20   Monsters of the year
go blank, are scattered back,
can't bear this march of three.

    —And the three have passed, vanished in the crowd
    (yet not vanished, for in their arms they wind
25   the life of men and beasts, and music,
    laughter ringing them round like a guard)
    at the end of this winter's day.

Questions

42.   Look at lines 1—8.

By referring to **one** example of language, explain how the poet creates a sense of joy.   **2**

43.   Look at lines 11—14.

By referring to **one** example of language, explain how the poet suggests the idea of innocence.

2

44.   Look at lines 15—22.

By referring to **two** examples of language, explain how the poet makes it clear that the group of three represents a strong force.   **4**

45.   Look at lines 23—27.

By referring to **two** examples of language, explain how the poet creates a positive ending to the poem.

4

46.   By referring to this poem and to at least one other by Morgan, show how setting is an important feature of his poetry.

8

[Turn over

OR

Text 3 — Poetry

If you choose this text you may not attempt a question on Poetry in Section 2.

Read the poem below and then attempt the following questions.

Aunt Julia **by Norman MacCaig**

Aunt Julia spoke Gaelic
very loud and very fast.
I could not answer her —
I could not understand her.

5   She wore men's boots
when she wore any.
— I can see her strong foot,
stained with peat,
paddling with the treadle of the spinningwheel
10   while her right hand drew yarn
marvellously out of the air.

Hers was the only house
where I've lain at night
in the absolute darkness
15   of a box bed, listening to
crickets being friendly.

She was buckets
and water flouncing into them.
She was winds pouring wetly
20   round house-ends.
She was brown eggs, black skirts
and a keeper of threepennybits
in a teapot.

Aunt Julia spoke Gaelic
25   very loud and very fast.
By the time I had learned
a little, she lay
silenced in the absolute black
of a sandy grave
30   at Luskentyre. But I hear her still, welcoming me
with a seagull's voice
across a hundred yards
of peatscrapes and lazybeds
and getting angry, getting angry
35   with so many questions
unanswered.

Questions

47. Look at lines 1—4.

By referring to **one** example of language, explain how the poet creates a clear sense of frustration.

2

48. Look at lines 5—23.

By referring to **two** examples of language, explain how the poet makes clear what Aunt Julia represents.

4

49. Look at lines 26—30 ("By the . . . Luskentyre").

By referring to **two** examples of language, explain how the poet creates a sad tone.

4

50. Look at lines 30—36 ("But I . . . unanswered").

How effective do you find these lines as a conclusion to the poem? You should refer to **one** example from these lines, and to the language **and/or** ideas of the rest of the poem.

2

51. By referring to this poem and to at least one other by MacCaig, show how being separated from people **and/or** things is an important idea in his poetry.

8

[Turn over

OR

Text 4 — Poetry

If you choose this text you may not attempt a question on Poetry in Section 2.

Read the poem below and then attempt the following questions.

Bed **by Jackie Kay**

> She is that guid tae me so she is
> an Am a burden tae her, I know Am ur.
> Stuck here in this big blastit bed
> year in, year oot, ony saint wuid complain.
>
> 5   There's things she has tae dae fir me
> A' wish she didnae huv tae dae.
> Am her wean noo, wey ma great tent o' nappy,
> an champed egg in a cup, an mashed tattie.
>
> Aw the treats A' used tae gie her,
> 10   she's gieing me. A' dinny ken whit happened.
> We dinny talk any mair. Whether it's jist
> the blethers ha been plucked oot o' us
>
> an Am here like some skinny chicken,
> ma skin aw bubbles and dots and spots,
> 15   loose flap noo (an yet as a young wuman
> A' took pride in ma guid smooth skin.)
>
> Aw A' dae is sit an look oot this windae.
> A've seen hale generations graw up
> an simmer doon fray this same windae —
> 20   that's no seen a lick o' paint fir donkeys.
>
> The Kerrs have disappeared, but the last
> Campbells ur still here so Am telt —
> tho' hauf the time A' dinny believe her:
> A've no seen ony Campbell in a lang time.
>
> 25   My dochter says 'Awright mother?'
> haunds me a thin broth or puried neep
> an A say 'Aye fine,' an canny help
> the great heaving sigh that comes oot
>
> my auld loose lips, nor ma crabbit tut,
> 30   nor ma froon when A' pu' ma cardie tight
> aroon ma shooders fir the night drawin in.
> Am jist biding time so am ur.
>
> Time is whit A' hauld between
> the soft bits o' ma thumbs,
> 35   the skeleton underneath ma night goon;
> aw the while the glaring selfish moon
>
> lights up this drab wee prison.
> A'll be gone and how wull she feel?
> No that Am saying A' want her guilty.
> 40   No that Am saying Am no grateful.

Page twenty-four

Questions

52.   Look at lines 1—12.

By referring to **two** examples of language, explain how the poet makes it clear that the speaker is unhappy with her current situation.

4

53.   Look at lines 13—20.

By referring to **two** examples of language, explain how the poet gives a clear impression of the negative aspects of old age.

4

54.   Look at lines 21—31.

By referring to **one** example of language, explain how the poet suggests that the speaker's relationship with her daughter is problematic.

2

55.   Look at lines 32—40.

Using your own words as far as possible, explain the speaker's thoughts about what her life has become. You should make **two** key points in your answer.

2

56.   By referring to this poem and to at least one other by Kay, show how she explores important changes in people's lives.

8

[END OF SECTION 1]

[Turn over

SECTION 2 — CRITICAL ESSAY — 20 marks

Attempt ONE question from the following genres — Drama, Prose, Poetry, Film and Television Drama, or Language.

Your answer must be on a different genre from that chosen in Section 1.

You should spend approximately 45 minutes on this Section.

DRAMA

> *Answers to questions in this part should refer to the text and to such relevant features as characterisation, key scene(s), structure, climax, theme, plot, conflict, setting . . .*

1. Choose a play in which there is conflict.

   Describe the conflict and by referring to the playwright's use of dramatic techniques, explain fully how the conflict develops.

2. Choose a play in which there is a scene that can be described as a turning point.

   Briefly describe what happens in this scene, and by referring to appropriate dramatic techniques, go on to explain why the scene is important to the play as a whole.

PROSE

> *Answers to questions in this part should refer to the text and to such relevant features as characterisation, setting, language, key incident(s), climax, turning point, plot, structure, narrative technique, theme, ideas, description . . .*

3. Choose a novel **or** a short story **or** a work of non-fiction which deals with an important issue or theme.

   By referring to appropriate techniques, show how the issue or theme is explored.

4. Choose a novel **or** a short story **or** a work of non-fiction which has a memorable character/person, place or event.

   By referring to appropriate techniques, explain how the writer makes the character/person, place or event memorable.

POETRY

Answers to questions in this part should refer to the text and to such relevant features as word choice, tone, imagery, structure, content, rhythm, rhyme, theme, sound, ideas . . .

5. Choose a poem which has a strong message.

   Consider the whole poem, and by referring to poetic techniques explain how the strong message is explored.

6. Choose a poem which creates a particular mood or atmosphere.

   By referring to poetic techniques, show how the poet creates this particular mood or atmosphere.

FILM AND TELEVISION DRAMA

Answers to questions in this part should refer to the text and to such relevant features as use of camera, key sequence, characterisation, mise-en-scène, editing, setting, music/sound, special effects, plot, dialogue . . .

7. Choose a scene or a sequence from a film or TV drama* which has a powerful impact on the audience.

   By referring to appropriate techniques, explain how the director creates this impact.

8. Choose a film or TV drama* which explores an important issue.

   By referring to appropriate techniques, explain how the director presents the issue in the film/TV drama as a whole.

* "TV drama" includes a single play, a series or a serial.

[Turn over

LANGUAGE

> *Answers to questions in this part should refer to the text and to such relevant features as register, accent, dialect, slang, jargon, vocabulary, tone, abbreviation . . .*

9. Consider the use of persuasive language in one or more advertisements that you have studied.

By referring to appropriate language techniques, explain how language is used effectively.

10. Consider the language used by two groups of people who are different in an important way. For example, they may be different in age, be from different places, or have different jobs.

By referring to specific examples, explain how language differences are important.

[END OF SECTION 2]

[END OF QUESTION PAPER]

NATIONAL 5

Answers

NATIONAL 5 ENGLISH 2015

READING FOR UNDERSTANDING, ANALYSIS AND EVALUATION

1. Candidates should explain why the first paragraph is an effective opening for the passage.

    Any three points from:

    *   It shows/introduces/explains/describes/connects to
    *   the idea (fight-flight-freeze)/theme/focus of the text/the rat
    *   creates interest/shock/pathos/drama.

    Also accept:

    *   reference to second person/"you"
    *   with chatty/informal tone
    *   single word/minor sentence/short sentence/"Ferociously!"
    *   series of short sentences.

2. **Glosses of both words:**

    *   "deeply" eg very/completely/profoundly
    *   "ingrained" eg embedded/fixed/rooted/established/ intuitive/natural/instinctive/in a long standing fashion.

3. Candidates should explain in their own words two aspects of "danger" or "threat" for two past experiences and two present experiences, from lines 14–21.

    Past – glosses of two:

    *   "head-on" eg direct/face to face
    *   "regularly" eg frequent
    *   "predators ...animal" eg creatures (which wanted to harm/kill us)
    *   "predators ...human kind" eg others like us (wanted to harm/kill us, eg through wars)
    *   accept example of predator
    *   "to life or limb" eg real physical harm.

    Present – glosses of two:

    *   "artificial" eg non-physical/psychological
    *   "to ego" eg to pride/self-esteem/vanity
    *   "to livelihood" eg to job/earnings
    *   "(consequences of) messing up" eg doing it wrong
    *   gloss of "taking exam"
    *   gloss of "giving a speech"
    *   gloss of "taking a penalty".

4. Referring to lines 22–37, candidate should summarise using their own words some of the changes in the body which occur with the response.

    Changes – glosses of:

    *   "acceleration of heart ... function" eg the heart beats more quickly
    *   "acceleration of ... lung function" eg breath comes faster
    *   "there is paling and flushing" eg the skin changes colour
    *   "there is an inhibition of stomach action, such that digestion almost completely ceases" eg the intestines work less
    *   "there is a constriction (of blood vessels)" eg (blood vessels) narrow
    *   "there is a freeing up of metabolic energy sources (fat and glycogen)" eg feel more energetic
    *   "there is a dilation (of the pupils)" eg the eyes widen/expand/enlarge
    *   "a relaxation of the bladder" eg waterworks loosen
    *   "perception narrows" eg concentration is (more) focused
    *   "shaking"/"trembling" eg shuddering or quaking or similar
    *   "prime (the muscles)" eg prepare/ready (the muscles)
    *   "increase body strength" eg become stronger
    *   "increase ... blood pressure" eg higher (blood pressure)
    *   "(become) hyper-vigilant" eg more alert/pay more attention
    *   "(adrenalin) pumping like crazy" eg increase (in adrenalin)
    *   "taut" eg tense/tightened
    *   "pumped" eg ready.

5. The candidate must offer an explanation on how the sentence "How to deal with these responses?" in line 44 provides an appropriate link at this point of the passage.

    *   "These responses" looks back
    *   "How"/"to deal" or question (mark) looks forward

    or

    *   "These responses" looks back
    *   to actions of team-mates or inner dialogue

    or

    *   "How"/"to deal" or question (mark) looks forward
    *   to identification of strategy (may quote "reflection")

    or

    *   reference to the ideas in the text before the link
    *   reference to the ideas in the text after the link.

6. By referring to lines 50–54, the candidate must explain **two** examples of the writer's word choice which demonstrate the "benefit" of the response.

    Any two points from:

    *   "huge" eg considerable
    *   "therapeutic" eg it helps
    *   "It takes the edge off" eg it makes us calmer
    *   "(It makes a ... bewildering reaction) into a comprehensible one" eg (it turns a baffling/puzzling reaction) into one which we understand
    *   "liberation" eg freeing
    *   "(liberation) from tyranny" eg from oppression
    *   "pressure" eg stress.

7. The candidate should explain the attitude of top athletes to pressure, and how two examples of the language used make this attitude clear with reference to lines 55–61.

Identification of attitude, eg pressure can be positive/beneficial.

Possible answers include:

- "paradoxical" /reference to paradox eg emphasises that expectation is worse than reality
- "Pressure is not a problem" eg bluntly states attitude
- "privilege" eg shows that this is something positive
- colon to introduce motto/mantra
- reference to alliteration eg accentuates the positive
- semi-colon after "problem" complements the balance
- balance/(idea of) antithesis of "Pressure ... privilege" draws attention to the bilateral nature
- example(s) cited of famous sportsmen suggests agreement
- "perfectly open" suggests acceptance
- reference to "but" starting sentence emphasises the contrast
- "great pride" emphasises how good they feel
- "facing up to them" shows positive attitude to confronting them
- "they didn't see these ... as signs of weakness" provides a clear statement
- "They created mechanisms" suggests coping strategies
- "grow" emphasises a chance to develop
- "seized (every opportunity)" shows they are keen
- repetition of "They" at the start of a sentence/parallel structure shows affirmative nature of the attitude.

8. The candidate should fully explain using their own words why the advice to "grab" the opportunity might at first seem strange by referring to lines 62–67.

Any three points from:

Then

Glosses of:

- "you will feel uncomfortable" eg you will find it awkward/unpleasant/unnerving
- "your stomach will knot" eg you will feel physically stressed
- "at the moment of truth, you will wish to be anywhere else in the world" eg at the critical/vital time you would wish you were not doing it
- "a nation's expectations on their shoulders" eg much is being hoped for you/pressure is applied/your patriotism is under test.

9. The candidate should pick an expression from the final paragraph (lines 68–71) and show how it helps to contribute to an effective conclusion to the passage.

Reference to an expression from earlier in the article should be made.

Possible answers include:

- "paradoxical" eg repeats word used earlier (line 55)
- "you will grow, learn and mature"eg revisits actual words "grow" (line 56) or "learnt" (line 57) or ideas of athletes profiting from the experience
- "on the football pitch" eg refers back to lines 9–12 or the title
- "in the office" eg refers back to "job interview" (line 45) or "at work" (lines 19–20)
- "fluff your lines" eg refers back to "giving a speech" (line 17)
- "if you miss" eg refers back to "taking a penalty" (line 17).

CRITICAL READING

SECTION 1 — Scottish Text

SCOTTISH TEXT — DRAMA

Text 1 — Drama — *Bold Girls* by Rona Munro

1. Candidates should show an understanding of the key events in this scene. Although the scene is short, many points are revealed here.

Candidates should deal with four separate points.

Possible answers include:

- Marie says she does not know how Cassie coped with Joe's affairs
- Marie displays an idealised view of her relationship with Michael
- Cassie seems to be preparing herself to confess her affair to Marie
- Cassie reacts against her environment
- Marie assures her there are things to look forward to
- Cassie says she is leaving
- Marie is shocked
- Cassie talks about her mother's idealised treatment of the men-folk in prison
- Cassie admits to stealing money from Nora by exploiting her lack of knowledge re the price of fruit
- Cassie shows humour/sarcasm in describing her predicament
- Cassie shows realism
- Marie shows her concern.

2. Candidates should show understanding of the attitudes of Marie.

Marie feels that men can be untrustworthy.

Marie has a romantic/idealised view of her relationship with Michael.

Candidates should refer to the dialogue and quotation is expected to support the argument.

1 mark for relevant quotation selected.

1 mark for appropriate comment about the attitude it reveals.

Possible answers include:

- "I don't know how you coped with all Joe's carry on." plus comment
- "You were the martyr there, Cassie" plus comment
- "I couldn't have stood that, just the lying to you" plus comment

- "It'll tear the heart out of me but tell me, just tell me the truth 'cause I'd want to know." plus comment
- "I never worried." plus comment
- "he was like my best friend" plus comment
- "that's what I miss most. The crack. The sharing." plus comment.

3. Candidates should demonstrate understanding of at least two aspects of Cassie's mood.

1 mark for selection of relevant reference.

1 mark for appropriate comment.

Cassie is in a reflective mood at the start of the extract. Her replies are short and monosyllabic/"It gave me peace."

She becomes more hesitant/regretful as indicated by the ellipsis/"Marie…"

She becomes angry and kicks the ground she stands on/"Aw Jesus I hate this place!"/she uses an exclamation

She makes a stand/she becomes defiant "I'm leaving"

She is sullen/belligerent She does not elaborate/"Cassie says nothing"

She complains at length about the way Joe and Martin are treated by Nora. She becomes sarcastic/"…she can spoil them with fruit…"

Sarcastic/bitter "I'll bring her home something that looks and smells like the Botanic Gardens…"

She becomes emphatic (about her plans to leave) "I've two hundred pounds saved. I'm going."

She then criticises herself (for stealing from Nora) "It's desperate isn't it? Thirty-five years old and she's stealing from her mummy's purse."

4. Candidates should discuss the treatment of gender in this extract and in at least one other scene from the play.

Points likely to be made about women include:

- Women take care of domestic work
- They struggle to make ends meet
- They support their friends
- They look after the children
- They do not have the same "social" freedom as men
- They support their men in prison
- They live with the threat of paramilitary/domestic violence.

Points likely to be made about men include:

- Men are more likely to be imprisoned
- Men imprisoned for paramilitary activities are highly regarded by their community
- Men have more "social freedom"
- Men "con" each other
- Men do not carry out domestic chores
- Men are more likely to commit acts of domestic violence.

Candidates may choose to answer in **bullet points** in this final question, or write a number of linked statements. There is **no requirement** to write a "mini essay".

Up to 2 marks can be achieved for identifying elements of **commonality** as identified in the question.

A further 2 marks can be achieved for **reference to the extract given**.

4 additional marks can be awarded for similar references to **at least one other text/part of the text** by the writer.

In practice this means:

Identification of commonality (eg: theme, central relationship, importance of setting, use of imagery, development in characterisation, use of personal experience, use of narrative style, or any other key element…)

from the extract:

1 × relevant reference to technique

1 × appropriate comment

or

1 × relevant reference to idea

1 × appropriate comment

or

1 × relevant reference to feature

1 × appropriate comment

or

1 × relevant reference to text

1 × appropriate comment

(maximum of 2 marks only for discussion of extract)

from **at least one other text/part of the text:**

as above (× 2) for **up to 4 marks**

Text 2 — Drama — *Sailmaker* by Alan Spence

5. Any two points to summarise the situation for 1 mark each.

Possible answers include:

- Alec's mother/Davie's wife has died
- Alec is beginning to come to terms with his mother's death
- Davie is struggling to cope with his grief/the death of his wife
- They are getting the house ready for visitors after the funeral.

6. Candidates should refer to **both** the weather and the setting for full marks.

1 mark for reference.

1 mark for comment.

Possible answers include:

Weather

- "breeze was warm"/"the breeze touched my cheek"/"sun shone"/"glinted"/"clouds moving across"
- Reflects Alec's feeling that his mother has gone to heaven/is safe
- "wee patch of clear blue"
- Patch of blue symbolises his mother going to heaven/a sign from her to reassure him.

Setting

- "ordinary"/"Nothing had changed" in contrast to the enormity of their loss

- "grey tenements"/"middens ... dustbins ... spilled ashes"/"broken glass"
- Setting is drab/miserable reflects their feelings of despair/depression/bereavement/poverty
- Evidence of rubbish/vandalism suggests lack of care his mother is now in a better place away from here
- "wee boy playing mouth organ"
- Notes on the mouth-organ sound like a bugle call as his mother leaves this world and enters heaven/reflects feelings of sadness.

7. Candidates should clearly identify how Davie is coping with his current situation.

   Candidates should support their responses with quotation and/or reference.

   1 mark for reference.

   1 mark for comment.

   Possible answers include:

   Supporting evidence:

   - Short sentence(s) to start speech Davie is trying to keep busy to avoid thinking
   - Long sentence with no punctuation reflects Davie's mind – he is trying to do lots of things to avoid stopping and thinking
   - Repetition of "nearly"/2nd time with italics for emphasis suggests he can never actually manage to forget
   - "Christ" use of blasphemy suggests the strength of his feeling
   - Use of 2nd person pronoun "ye"/"you" – to distance himself from situation/make it more general rather than face up to it
   - List of things Davie does reflects him carrying out a number of tasks to avoid thinking
   - "whole minutes" emphasises how often he is thinking about his wife
   - "hit(s) ye" – suggests the almost physical nature of his pain.

8. Candidates should focus on the language used by the characters.

   2 marks for identification of two differences.

   Possible answers include:

   - Alec speaks in English, Davie speaks in Scots
   - Alec's words are in the past tense, Davie's words are in the present tense
   - Alec's words are in sentences, Davie's sentences lack punctuation
   - Alec's sentences are short(er), Davie's are long(er)
   - Alec's sentences are (more) structured, Davie's are (more) unstructured/chaotic
   - Alec's words are more descriptive/poetic, Davie's words are more matter of fact/down to earth
   - Alec's words act as narration, Davie's words act as the speech of a character.

9. Candidates should identify the way the father-son relationship is developed in this extract and elsewhere in the play.

Possible comments from elsewhere include:

- Admiration at start of play
- Spending the bursary money
- Drinking/gambling issues
- Lack of trust
- Neglect/physical abuse
- Acceptance of going separate ways
- Burning yacht etc a resolution/more positive
- Contrast with Billy and Ian's relationship.

Candidates may choose to answer in **bullet points** in this final question, or write a number of linked statements. There is **no requirement** to write a 'mini essay'.

Up to 2 marks can be achieved for identifying elements of **commonality** as identified in the question.

A further 2 marks can be achieved for **reference to the extract** given.

4 additional marks can be awarded for similar references to **at least one other text/part of the text** by the writer.

<u>In practice this means:</u>

Identification of commonality (eg: theme, central relationship, importance of setting, use of imagery, development in characterisation, use of personal experience, use of narrative style, or any other key element...)

from the extract:

1 × relevant reference to technique

1 × appropriate comment

or

1 × relevant reference to idea

1 × appropriate comment

or

1 × relevant reference to feature

1 × appropriate comment

or

1 × relevant reference to text

1 × appropriate comment

(maximum of 2 marks only for discussion of extract)

from **at least one other text/part of the text:**

as above (× 2) for **up to 4 marks**

Text 3 — Drama — *Tally's Blood* by Ann Marie de Mambro

10. Candidates need to cover four separate points to achieve full marks.

    Possible answers include:

    - Her father had arranged for her to marry someone else (Ferdinando, who had a lot of land)
    - Then she met Massimo and fell in love at first sight/very quickly
    - Her father wouldn't allow it and locked her in a room
    - Massimo climbed up to rescue her
    - They spent the evening together hiding up a tree
    - To deliberately cause a scandal
    - So they would have to be allowed to get married.

11. Candidates should deal with four of the points suggested. For full marks they must show some **change** in Rosinella's thoughts.

    1 mark for reference.

    1 mark for comment.

    Possible answers include:

    - At first she is *"Cagey"* suggesting she is reluctant initially

    - Then she starts *"Getting into it"* suggesting she is starting to take some pleasure in it

    - She is *"Undecided about whether or not to tell"* suggesting she is unsure about what to do

    - *"but then does so with glee"* suggesting that she is taking delight in it

    - *"Enjoying it now"* suggests she is taking pleasure from it

    - *"Mimics the sound"* suggests she is telling the story with some conviction

    - By the end she is *"Moved by her story"* suggesting she is completely involved.

12. 1 mark for identification of tone.

    1 mark for comment.

    Possible tones might include:

    nostalgic, romantic, reflective, wistful, humorous, etc.

    Any reasonable justification for answer.

13. Candidates are only being asked to identify examples from the extract.

    Possible examples include:

    "wee", "awfy", "they" (instead of those), "no" (instead of not), "faither", "wean", "hen", "ma" (instead of my).

    Any two for 1 mark each.

14. Candidates should discuss how romantic relationships are developed in this extract and elsewhere in the play.

    Possible comments from elsewhere include:

    - Comment on forbidden relationships

    - Lucia and Hughie are childhood friends who end up in a relationship

    - Franco and Bridget's difficult relationship

    - Rosinella and Massimo's elopement and enduring relationship.

    Candidates may choose to answer in **bullet points** in this final question, or write a number of linked statements. There is **no requirement** to write a "mini essay".

    Up to 2 marks can be achieved for identifying elements of **commonality** as identified in the question.

    A further 2 marks can be achieved for **reference to the extract given.**

    4 additional marks can be awarded for similar references to **at least one other text/part of the text** by the writer.

    <u>In practice this means:</u>

    Identification of commonality (eg: theme, central relationship, importance of setting, use of imagery, development in characterisation, use of personal experience, use of narrative style, or any other key element...)

    from the extract:

    1 × relevant reference to technique

    1 × appropriate comment

    or

    1 × relevant reference to idea

    1 × appropriate comment

    or

    1 × relevant reference to feature

    1 × appropriate comment

    or

    1 × relevant reference to text

    1 × appropriate comment

    (maximum of 2 marks only for discussion of extract)

    from **at least one other text/part of the text:**

    as above (× 2) for **up to 4 marks**

Text 1 — Prose — *The Cone-Gatherers* by Robin Jenkins

15. Any two for one mark each.

    Possible answers include:

    - sensitive

    - gentle

    - empathy with animals

    - clumsy in his movements (when not in the trees)

    - upset.

16. 1 mark for identification.

    1 mark for comment.

    Possible answers include:

    - "Icy sweat of hatred" plus comment

    - "His gun aimed at the (feebleminded) hunchback" plus comment

    - "The obscene squeal of the killed dwarf" plus comment

    - "Noose of disgust and despair" plus comment.

17. 1 mark for any one quotation.

    1 mark for comment.

    Possible answers include:

    - Sea imagery – "sea of branches"/"fantastic sea"/"quiet as fish"/"seaweed"/"submarine monsters" plus comment

    - "bronzen brackens" plus comment

    - "the overspreading tree of revulsion" plus comment.

18. Candidates must show Duror's feelings before and after.

    Before the arrival he felt safe/happy/secure/peaceful/calm, etc there.

    After the arrival he felt it had been spoiled/ruined, etc for him.

19. Candidates should discuss how the character of Calum is presented in this extract and elsewhere in the novel.

    Possible answers from elsewhere include:

    - Calum's gentleness

    - Examples of descriptions of Calum's gentleness

    - References to Calum's clumsiness when he is not in the trees

- Detailed description of nature (and how it relates to Calum) which occurs throughout the novel.

Candidates may choose to answer in **bullet points** in this final question, or write a number of linked statements. There is **no requirement** to write a "mini essay".

Up to 2 marks can be achieved for identifying elements of **commonality** as identified in the question.

A further 2 marks can be achieved for **reference to the extract given.**

4 additional marks can be awarded for similar references to **at least one other text/part of the text** by the writer.

In practice this means:

Identification of commonality (eg: theme, central relationship, importance of setting, use of imagery, development in characterisation, use of personal experience, use of narrative style, or any other key element…)

from the extract:

1 × relevant reference to technique

1 × appropriate comment

or

1 × relevant reference to idea

1 × appropriate comment

or

1 × relevant reference to feature

1 × appropriate comment

or

1 × relevant reference to text (1)

1 × appropriate comment (1)

(maximum of 2 marks only for discussion of extract)

from **at least one other text/part of the text:**

as above (× 2) for **up to 4 marks**

Text 2 — Prose — *The Testament of Gideon Mack* by James Robertson

20. 1 mark for each identification of aspect.

    Possible answers include:
    - Two faced/duplicitous
    - rebellious
    - made himself inconspicuous
    - clever/crafty.

21. **(a)** 1 mark for reference.

    1 mark for comment.

    Possible answers include:
    - "went through with the whole business" suggesting difficulty or hardship or lack of enjoyment
    - "a rigorous undertaking" suggesting difficulty or hardship
    - "an even greater commitment" suggesting a lot is being asked of him
    - "you would have to go a long way...but I did" suggesting his task was harder or that he achieved more than others
    - "dissected and deciphered" suggesting the in-depth nature of the work.

(b) 1 mark for reference.

1 mark for comment.

Possible answers include:
- "think of this" – use of command to get the reader's attention/force the reader to consider the task
- repetition of "the nature of" to emphasise the full extent of the task
- listing to emphasise the sheer number of topics covered
- repetition in "many, many hours" to emphasise the time spent on this.

22. 1 mark for comment on the relationship.

1 mark for supporting evidence.

Possible answers include:
- grudging admiration – "respect"
- understanding from Mack – "I was there with him"
- still a lack of closeness between them – "a part of me was keeping its distance".

23. Candidates should discuss how the theme of deception is explored in this extract and elsewhere in the novel.

Possible comments from elsewhere include:
- he became a minister although he doesn't believe in God
- he continues to be hypocritical within his profession
- the first person narration allows the reader to see the inner thoughts versus the outward appearance
- various individual scenes of duplicity throughout the novel, any two examples.

Candidates may choose to answer in **bullet points** in this final question, or write a number of linked statements. There is **no requirement** to write a "mini essay".

Up to 2 marks can be achieved for identifying elements of **commonality** as identified in the question.

A further 2 marks can be achieved for **reference to the extract given.**

4 additional marks can be awarded for similar references to **at least one other text/part of the text** by the writer.

In practice this means:

Identification of commonality (eg: theme, central relationship, importance of setting, use of imagery, development in characterisation, use of personal experience, use of narrative style, or any other key element…)

from the extract:

1 × relevant reference to technique

1 × appropriate comment

or

1 × relevant reference to idea

1 × appropriate comment

or

1 × relevant reference to feature

1 × appropriate comment

or

1 × relevant reference to text

1 × appropriate comment

(maximum of 2 marks only for discussion of extract)

from **at least one other text/part of the text**:

as above (× 2) for **up to 4 marks**

Text 3 — Prose — *Kidnapped* by Robert Louis Stevenson

24. Four points to be made.

    One mark for each point.

    Possible answers include:

    - David arrives in/near Edinburgh
    - David asks for directions to Cramond
    - David sees/hears the redcoats
    - David asks/talks to a man with a cart about the house of Shaws
    - David receives negative response from the carter
    - David asks/talks to a barber about the house of Shaws
    - David receives negative response from the barber
    - David is left concerned.

25. There should be an understanding that David believes that it is the juxtaposition between his simple, grubby clothes which jarred with his asking about – what he thought was – a grand house such as the Shaws.

    A gloss of:

    "At first I thought the plainness of my appearance, in my country habit, and that all dusty from the road," (1 mark)

    "consorted ill with the greatness of the place to which I was bound." (1 mark)

26. (a) 1 mark for statement of mood in opening paragraph.

    1 mark for example of writer's use of language in opening paragraph.

    1 mark for comment on language.

    Possible answers include:

    - mood – optimistic, happy, content, etc.

    Word choice:

    - "pleasure" have a great liking/desire
    - "wonder" – as to marvel at a great spectacle
    - "beheld" – to observe something of great impact
    - "pride" delight/joy at the sight
    - "merry (music)" – joyful/happy.

    Metaphor:

    - "the pride of life seemed to mount into my brain" to be at the forefront of the mind/to be directly connected to the mind in a powerful way.

    Alliteration:

    - "merry music" repeated "m" sound has a length which pleasant, soft, jaunty and childlike in its alliterative use.

    (b) 1 mark for statement of mood in final paragraph.

    1 mark for example of writer's use of language in final paragraph.

    1 mark for comment on language.

    Possible answers include:

    - mood – pessimistic, confused, perturbed, etc.

Word choice:

- "illusions" – deceptive/misconception
- "indistinct" – unclear
- "accusations" – negative connotations of illegal actions
- "fancy" imagination not reality
- "start and stare" showing shock at the mention of Shaws (also could award marks for the sharp alliterative effect of the sibilance)
- "ill-fame" – of poor reputation.

Metaphor:

- "the blow this dealt to my illusions" – affected almost physically/violently as with a blow.

Sentence structure:

- use of two questions/placement of questions at end of paragraph emphasising doubt and confusion/climactic nature.

27. Candidates should discuss the development of David Balfour's character in this extract and elsewhere in the novel.

    Possible comments from elsewhere include:

    - becomes more adventurous
    - becomes more experienced
    - becomes more confident
    - any two specific points in the novel which show his development.

    Candidates may choose to answer in **bullet points** in this final question, or write a number of linked statements. There is **no requirement** to write a "mini essay".

    Up to 2 marks can be achieved for identifying elements of **commonality** as identified in the question.

    A further 2 marks can be achieved for **reference to the extract given.**

    4 additional marks can be awarded for similar references to **at least one other text/part of the text** by the writer.

    <u>In practice this means:</u>

    Identification of commonality (eg: theme, central relationship, importance of setting, use of imagery, development in characterisation, use of personal experience, use of narrative style, or any other key element...)

    from the extract:

    1 × relevant reference to technique

    1 × appropriate comment

    or

    1 × relevant reference to idea

    1 × appropriate comment

    or

    1 × relevant reference to feature

    1 × appropriate comment

    or

    1 × relevant reference to text

    1 × appropriate comment

    (maximum of 2 marks only for discussion of extract)

from **at least one other text/part of the text:**

as above (× 2) for **up to 4 marks**

Text 4 – Prose – *Mother and Son* by Iain Crichton Smith

28. Candidates should give 4 relevant points for 1 mark each.

    Possible answers include:

    • Constantly ridicules him – "always laughed at him"

    • Picks on him/highlights his faults persistently – "pecked cruelly at his defences"

    • Hates the power she has over him despite her frailty – "What is she anyway?"/"How can this thing....?"

    • Anger that she uses illness as a reason to behave as she does – "She's been ill...doesn't excuse her"

    • Anger that she is destroying his life – "she's breaking me up"

    • Also his chances of a life in the future – "if she dies...good for anyone."

    • Blames her for his loneliness/isolation from his peers – "shivered inside his loneliness"/"That would be the boys...".

29. 1 mark for reference.

    1 mark for comment.

    Possible examples/explanations:

    • "face had sharpened itself... quickness"/"pecking at....cruelly at his defences" – emphasises her sharpness/although small and frail like a bird has the capacity to destroy him

    • "some kind of animal"/"this thing" – makes her seem less than human

    • "breaking me up" – idea that she is destroying him

    • Description of his angry actions shows his feelings

    • "abrupt"/"savage"/shaking with anger towards her/"rage shook him" shows how angry he is

    • Use of questions/"How can this thing..."/"What is she anyway?" Emphasise the hateful thoughts he has towards her.

30. 1 mark for reference.

    1 mark for comment.

    Possible examples/explanations:

    • (sense of loneliness) "closed around him" feels engulfed by loneliness

    • "on a boat on the limitless ocean" feels adrift and alone in an endless sea

    • (compares this to his own home) "just as his house was on a limitless moorland" – gives sense of isolation.

31. 1 mark for reference.

    1 mark for comment.

    Possible answers include:

    • "Remember to clean the tray tomorrow"/mother's words are seen as provocative

    • "fighting back the anger" suggests rising emotion

    • "swept over him" overwhelming feelings

    • "He turned back to the bed." – it's a dramatic moment

    • (Repetition of) "smash" suggestion of potential violence

    • (Repetition of) "there was" creation of drama

    • Final short sentence makes for dramatic ending.

32. Candidates should discuss a character's realisation in this extract as well as at least one other character's realisation from at least one other story.

    Possible comments from other stories include:

    'The Telegram' – true destination of telegram, more understanding between the two women

    'The Red Door' – realisation of sense of freedom for main character

    'In Church' – realisation of futility of war

    'The Painter' – realisation of unpleasantness of community.

    Candidates may choose to answer in **bullet points** in this final question, or write a number of linked statements. There is **no requirement** to write a "mini essay".

    Up to 2 marks can be achieved for identifying elements of **commonality** as identified in the question.

    A further 2 marks can be achieved for **reference to the extract given.**

    4 additional marks can be awarded for similar references to **at least one other text/part of the text** by the writer.

    <u>In practice this means:</u>

    Identification of commonality (2) (eg: theme, central relationship, importance of setting, use of imagery, development in characterisation, use of personal experience, use of narrative style, or any other key element...)

    from the extract:

    1 × relevant reference to technique

    1 × appropriate comment

    or

    1 × relevant reference to idea

    1 × appropriate comment

    or

    1 × relevant reference to feature

    1 × appropriate comment

    or

    1 × relevant reference to text

    1 × appropriate comment

    (maximum of 2 marks only for discussion of extract)

    from **at least one other text/part of the text:**

    as above (× 2) for **up to 4 marks**

Text 5 – Prose – *All That Glisters* by Anne Donovan

33. Four separate points for one mark each.

    Possible answers include:

    • The family prepare for the funeral

    • Father's body put in parents' bedroom

    • Girl asked if she wants to see body

    • Girl has mixed feelings about seeing the body

    • Girl feels her mother is acting aloof

    • Girl gets dressed for funeral

    • Auntie Pauline reacts badly to girl's choice of outfit

- Memory of wearing dress for father
- Memory of father's approval.

34. 1 mark for reference.

1 mark for comment.

Possible answers include:

- "blur" unclear/many things happening/movement
- Movement of people "comin and goin" busy/confusing
- ("makin sandwiches" and "pourin oot glasses of whisky") for "men in overcoats" whom she doesn't recognise, perhaps distant or seldom seen relatives
- "makin sandwiches"/"pourin oot glasses of whisky" suggests endless hospitality
- reference to listing or use of commas suggests confusion of events or lack of clarity.

35. 1 mark for identification of feature.

Possible answers include:

- (Repeated) use of first person
- Use of parenthesis
- Use of question
- Use of Scots
- Use of colloquial language
- Long/rambling sentences.

36. 1 mark for reference.

1 mark for comment.

Possible answers include:

- "her face froze over" shows her disgust/astonishment
- Use of (rhetorical) question/"Whit the hell do you think you're daein?" shows shock/disapproval
- Use of (expletive)/"hell" shows anger
- Use of imperatives/"Go...get changed" shows her disapproval of the outfit
- Instructions/commands/insistence show her disapproval.

37. Candidates should discuss how the theme of relationships is explored in this extract and in at least one other story by Donovan.

Possible comments from other stories include:

'A Chitterin' Bite' – breakdown of two relationships, loss of friendship etc

'Zimmerobics' – relationships across generations

'Dear Santa'/'Away in a Manger' – mother-daughter relationships

Candidates may choose to answer in **bullet points** in this final question, or write a number of linked statements. There is **no requirement** to write a "mini essay".

Up to 2 marks can be achieved for identifying elements of **commonality** as identified in the question.

A further 2 marks can be achieved for **reference to the extract given**.

4 additional marks can be awarded for similar references to **at least one other text/part of the text** by the writer.

<u>In practice this means:</u>

Identification of commonality (eg: theme, central relationship, importance of setting, use of imagery, development in characterisation, use of personal experience, use of narrative style, or any other key element...)

from the extract:

1 × relevant reference to technique

1 × appropriate comment

or

1 × relevant reference to idea

1 × appropriate comment

or

1 × relevant reference to feature

1 × appropriate comment

or

1 × relevant reference to text

1 × appropriate comment

(maximum of 2 marks only for discussion of extract)

from **at least one other text/part of the text:**

as above (× 2) for **up to 4 marks**

Text 1 — Poetry — *Valentine* by Carol Ann Duffy

38. Two marks can be awarded for two main ideas or concerns shown in first two lines.

Only one mark should be awarded for one main idea or concern.

Possible answers include:

- (The unsatisfactory nature of) traditional Valentine gifts
- The rejection of a clichéd/conventional view of love
- Offering of an alternative
- The need to be honest/truthful about love
- The importance of recognising the mundane/unpleasant aspects of love.

39. Four marks can be awarded for two examples of language used to create a positive view of love.

1 mark for example.

1 mark for comment.

Possible answers include:

- The word choice of "moon" suggests romance/is a conventional romantic symbol
- The word choice of "promised" suggests commitment/guarantee that love will flourish
- The word choice of "light" links to "moon" to reinforce romantic associations/has positive connotations linked to goodness or truth
- The word choice of "careful" has connotations of tenderness
- The comparison of removing the skin of an onion to "undressing" adds seductive/sexual element.

40. Two marks can be awarded for one example of language used to create a negative view of love.

1 mark for example.

1 mark for comment.

Possible answers include:

- "blind you with tears" suggests upset/pain

- "blind" suggests the distortion/lack of clarity cc
- "a wobbling photo of grief" suggests unsettling/distorting nature of love Accept comments on "photo" or "grief" itself
- The personification of "kiss" as "fierce"/word choice of "fierce" suggests danger/threat/aggression
- "will stay on your lips" (to suggest the lingering taste of the onion) suggests the difficulty of escaping a relationship
- The word choice of "possessive" suggests jealousy/desire to control
- The juxtaposition of "possessive" and "faithful" undermines the normally positive view of commitment
- The inclusion/qualification of "for as long" suggests that the commitment will not last.

41. Candidates should show understanding of the term "conclusion" and how the content of the last stanza continues ideas and/or language from the earlier stanzas.

    2 marks for reference to the final stanza referring back to earlier in the poem.

    Possible answers include:

    - (The imperative) "Take it" continues the portrayal of the speaker as commanding/insistent
    - (The imperative) "Take it" concludes a series of imperatives to suggest the listener's reluctance to accept the gift
    - "platinum" suggests the enduring value of love (despite the negative features highlighted)
    - "loops" suggests never ending commitment/constraint/control highlighted earlier
    - "shrink" reinforces the claustrophobic/constraining nature of marriage
    - The comparison of the inner rings of the onion to a "wedding ring" continues the subverting of conventional symbols of love/reinforces the constraining nature of marriage
    - The parody of a wedding proposal in " if you like "continues the subverting of conventional romantic symbols
    - The positioning of "Lethal" in a line of its own/the word choice of "Lethal" develops/reinforces previous examples of aggression
    - "cling"/repetition of "cling" links back to the "possessive" nature of love mentioned earlier
    - "knife" reinforces love as menacing or dangerous.

42. Candidates should show awareness of the ideas and/or language of this poem and at least one other poem by Duffy.

    Possible comments from other poems include:

    "Havisham" – pain of relationship breaking down

    "Originally" – relationship with environment/identity/self-knowledge

    "Ann Hathaway" – sexual relationship

    "War Photographer" – photographer's relationship with work/material

    "Mrs Midas" – breakdown in relationship/memories of good times.

Candidates may choose to answer in **bullet points** in this final question, or write a number of linked statements. There is **no requirement** to write a "mini essay".

Up to 2 marks can be achieved for identifying elements of **commonality** as identified in the question.

A further 2 marks can be achieved for **reference to the extract given.**

4 additional marks can be awarded for similar references to **at least one other text/part of the text** by the writer.

<u>In practice this means:</u>

Identification of commonality (eg: theme, central relationship, importance of setting, use of imagery, development in characterisation, use of personal experience, use of narrative style, or any other key element…)

from the extract:

1 × relevant reference to technique

1 × appropriate comment

or

1 × relevant reference to idea

1 × appropriate comment

or

1 × relevant reference to feature

1 × appropriate comment

or

1 × relevant reference to text

1 × appropriate comment

(maximum of 2 marks only for discussion of extract)

from **at least one other text/part of the text:**

as above (× 2) for **up to 4 marks**

Text 2 — Poetry — *Hyena* **by Edwin Morgan**

43. For full marks answers should make two clear points.

    One mark for each point. Own words required.

    Possible answers include:

    - Hyena is patient
    - Hyena is dangerous/threatening
    - Hyena is self-obsessed
    - Hyena is hungry and thirsty
    - Hunger makes hyena more threatening
    - Hyena must not be underestimated
    - Hyena may appear to be asleep but can pounce at any time.

44. Two references plus comments on two features used by the writer in these lines.

    1 mark for reference.

    1 mark for comment.

    Possible answers include:

    - "I have a rough coat" **or** "with dark spots like the bush-tufted plains of Africa" **or** "a shaggy bundle" – he is inelegant/scruffy
    - "crafty" he is sly/clever
    - "I sprawl … of gathered energy" eg he appears to be relaxed but is ready to pounce

- "I lope, I slaver" – he is ungainly/clumsy
- The list describes the hyena's movement, etc
- "I am a ranger" he scans the landscape for dead animals
- Reference to "I eat the dead" eg he profits by feeding on creatures already dead/lacks the dignity or skill of a hunter, etc
- Use of short sentences suggests threatening nature of hyena/his grim certainty, etc
- Use of repetition suggests threatening nature, etc
- Use of question suggests apparent confidence of hyena, etc.

45. 1 mark for reference to feature.

    1 mark for comment relating to tense, menacing atmosphere.

    Possible answers include:

- Use of questions to emphasise the hyena's slyness or power
- Use of euphemism as the hyena calls his howl his "song"
- Reference to aspects of setting/background, eg "moon pours hard and cold" suggests eerie place
- Use of short sentences to increase tension
- Conversational tone eg "Would you meet me there in the waste places?" creating false sense of friendliness
- "my golden supper" is a macabre image
- "I am not laughing" is a chilling statement
- "crowd of fangs" is threatening/dangerous
- "I am not laughing" could be seen as a threat/warning.

46. For 2 marks, candidates should refer to a feature of the last stanza and show how it effectively continues an idea/language feature from earlier in the poem.

    Possible answers include:

- "I am waiting" repeats opening line/reiterates that the hyena is always ready to feed on carrion/gives the poem a cyclical structure
- "I am crouching … till you are ready for me" recalls the hyena lying in wait in stanza one
- "My place is to pick you clean and leave your bones to the wind" brings the references to "you" throughout the poem to a macabre climax.

47. Candidates should show understanding of how Morgan uses word choice and/or imagery effectively to create a striking visual impression or scene in this poem and in at least one other poem.

    Possible comments on other poems include:

    "Good Friday" – clear sense of scene comes across with several visual references to the journey of the bus ("brakes violently," "lurches round into the sun," etc)

    "In the snack bar" – many references to place/scene throughout the poem

    "Trio" – winter/Christmas scene established through expressions such as "sharp winter evening," "under the Christmas lights," etc

    "Winter" – many references to place/scene throughout the poem

    "Slate" – many references to place/scene throughout the poem.

Candidates may choose to answer in **bullet points** in this final question, or write a number of linked statements. There is **no requirement** to write a "mini essay".

Up to 2 marks can be achieved for identifying elements of **commonality** as identified in the question.

A further 2 marks can be achieved for **reference to the extract given**.

4 additional marks can be awarded for similar references to **at least one other text/part of the text** by the writer.

In practice this means:

Identification of commonality (eg: theme, central relationship, importance of setting, use of imagery, development in characterisation, use of personal experience, use of narrative style, or any other key element…)

from the extract:

1 × relevant reference to technique

1 × appropriate comment

or

1 × relevant reference to idea

1 × appropriate comment

or

1 × relevant reference to feature

1 × appropriate comment

or

1 × relevant reference to text

1 × appropriate comment

(maximum of 2 marks only for discussion of extract)

from **at least one other text/part of the text:**

as above (× 2) for **up to 4 marks**

Text 3 — Poetry — *Visiting Hour* by Norman MacCaig

48. 1 mark for reference.

    1 mark for comment.

    Possible answers include:

- "The hospital smell combs my nostrils" suggests visit is familiar/unpleasant/overpowering smell/vivid sensory image
- "green and yellow corridors" suggests he finds visit unpleasant – connotations of colours/vivid sensory image
- "What seems a corpse" suggests he feels uncertainty/anxiety about visit
- "trundled" suggests he feels the patient is being treated impersonally/dehumanised
- "vanishes" suggests he is very aware of death as absolute/final
- "heavenward" suggests he is very aware of finality of death/religious questions
- "I will not feel, I will not feel, until I have to"/repetition here tries to delay/avoid emotions.

49. 1 mark for technique.

    1 mark for comment.

    Possible answers include:

- "walk lightly, swiftly" – repetition of adverbs admires nurses' ability to deal with stresses of nursing

- "here and up and down and there" – unusual word order lightens mood/emphasises number/activity of nurses
- "their slender waists miraculously carrying their burden" – word-choice/metaphor admires nurses' ability to deal with stresses/burden despite being small/light
- "miraculously" – word choice – religious connotations poet thinks nurses are angelic/have magical powers
- "so much pain, so/many deaths …/so many farewells" – Repetition of "so" suggests admiration for nurses who have to deal with pain and death frequently.

50. 1 mark for reference.

1 mark for comment.

Possible answers include:

- "white cave of forgetfulness" or gloss suggests curtains or sheets are impenetrable/patient is isolated or ignored/poet is excluded/patient herself cannot remember things
- "withered hand/trembles on its stalk" or gloss woman's body is dying/frail/weak
- "Eyes move behind eyelids too heavy to raise" or gloss impersonal description/suggests how ill/weak patient is
- "Arm wasted of colour" or gloss arm is pale, lifeless, useless, no longer functioning
- "glass fang" or gloss suggests vampire-like IV, emphasising the poet's grief and distress
- "not guzzling but giving" or gloss alliteration suggests poet first sees the transfusion as pointless but then realises it is keeping patient alive.

51. Candidates should discuss MacCaig's use of imagery in this poem and in at least one other poem.

Possible comments from other poems include:

"Assisi" – appropriate comments on eg "half-filled sack"; "clucking contentedly", etc

"Memorial" – appropriate comments on eg "carousel of language"; "sad music", etc

"Basking Shark" – appropriate comments on eg "tin-tacked with rain"; "roomsized monster with a matchbox brain", etc

"Sounds of the Day" – "black drums rolled"; "bangle of ice round your wrist", etc

"Aunt Julia" – "she was buckets"; "with a seagull's voice", etc.

Candidates may choose to answer in **bullet points** in this final question, or write a number of linked statements. There is **no requirement** to write a "mini essay".

Up to 2 marks can be achieved for identifying elements of **commonality** as identified in the question.

A further 2 marks can be achieved for **reference to the extract given.**

4 additional marks can be awarded for similar references to **at least one other text/part of the text** by the writer.

In practice this means:

Identification of commonality (eg: theme, central relationship, importance of setting, use of imagery,

development in characterisation, use of personal experience, use of narrative style, or any other key element…)

from the extract:

1 × relevant reference to technique

1 × appropriate comment

or

1 × relevant reference to idea

1 × appropriate comment

or

1 × relevant reference to feature

1 × appropriate comment

or

1 × relevant reference to text

1 × appropriate comment

(maximum of 2 marks only for discussion of extract)

from **at least one other text/part of the text:**

as above (× 2) for **up to 4 marks**

Text 4 — Poetry — *Divorce* by Jackie Kay

52. Candidates can refer to meaning or to techniques.

Two references to meaning 1 mark each.

1 mark for reference to technique.

1 mark for comment.

Possible answers include:

- She did not make a vow to stay together
- As her parents had done
- She wants out now
- She uses an emphatic tone
- She uses monosyllabic words
- She uses enjambment
- She uses a cliché
- She uses an ironic tone
- She uses negative language.

53. Candidates should make 3 distinct points for 3 marks.

Possible answers include:

- Gloss of "you never, ever said/a kind word" – mother was not positive/encouraging to her
- Gloss of "or a thank-you" – mother was ungrateful
- "tedious chores" – parents made the persona do hard/demanding housework
- "your breath smells like a camel," etc – father was (personally) repulsive
- "Are you in the cream puff," etc – father made sarcastic comments
- "Lady muck" – father put her down
- "I'd be better off in an orphanage" – emphasises how bad they are.

54. 1 mark for reference.

1 mark for comment.

Possible answers include:

- "faces turn up to the light" "(turn) up" **or** "light" suggest positivity, enlightenment

- "who speak in the soft murmur of rivers" suggests calmness/quiet
- "and never shout" suggests calm, quiet approach
- "stroke their children's cheeks" suggests love/gentleness/caring
- "sing in the colourful voices of rainbows, red to blue" suggests brightness/enjoyment/happiness/beauty/varied approach, etc.

55. 1 mark for identification of tone.

   1 mark for reference.

   1 mark for comment.

   Possible answers include:

   Humour:

   - "and quickly" – persona can't wait to get away from parents
   - "your breath smells like a camel" humorously unappealing/exaggeration/further reference to "gives me the hump"
   - "I would be better off in an orphanage" – humorous exaggeration.

   Despair:

   - reference to "there are things I cannot suffer any longer" – persona is at end of tether.

   Anger:

   - "I never chose you" – persona is angry with parents/fact that she is trapped.

   Dismissive:

   - reference to "I don't want to be your child"/"These parents are not you"/"not you" persona rejects parents.

   Admiration:

   - reference to "There are parents whose faces turn up to the light"/"There are parents who stroke their children's cheeks"/"sing in the colourful voices of rainbows", etc, the persona admires these parents and wishes hers could be more like them.

   Any other reasonable identification of a tone, plus reference, plus comment.

56. Candidates should discuss the theme of family relationships in this poem and at least one other poem by Jackie Kay.

   Possible comments on other poems include:

   "My Grandmother's Houses" – girl/grandmother

   "Lucozade" – mother/daughter

   "Gap Year" – mother/daughter

   "Bed" – mother/daughter

   "Keeping Orchids" – mother/daughter

   Candidates may choose to answer in **bullet points** in this final question, or write a number of linked statements. There is **no requirement** to write a "mini essay".

   Up to 2 marks can be achieved for identifying elements of **commonality** as identified in the question.

   A further 2 marks can be achieved for **reference to the extract given.**

4 additional marks can be awarded for similar references to **at least one other text/part of the text** by the writer.

In practice this means:

Identification of commonality (eg: theme, central relationship, importance of setting, use of imagery, development in characterisation, use of personal experience, use of narrative style, or any other key element…)

from the extract:

1 × relevant reference to technique

1 × appropriate comment

or

1 × relevant reference to idea

1 × appropriate comment

or

1 × relevant reference to feature

1 × appropriate comment

or

1 × relevant reference to text

1 × appropriate comment

(maximum of 2 marks only for discussion of extract)

from **at least one other text/part of the text:**

as above (× 2) for **up to 4 marks**

SECTION 2 – Critical Essay

Bands are not grades. The five bands are designed primarily to assist with placing each candidate response at an appropriate point on a continuum of achievement. Assumptions about final grades or association of final grades with particular bands should not be allowed to influence objective assessment.

	20–18	17–14	13–10	9–5	4–0
The candidate demonstrates:	• **a high degree of familiarity** with the text as a whole • **very good understanding** of the central concerns of the text • a line of thought that is **consistently** relevant to the task	• **familiarity** with the text as a whole • **good understanding** of the central concerns of the text • a line of thought that is **relevant** to the task	• **some familiarity** with the text as a whole • **some understanding** of the central concerns of the text • a line of thought that is **mostly relevant** to the task	• **familiarity with some aspects** of the text • **attempts** a line of thought **but this may lack relevance to the task**	Although such essays should be rare, in this category, the candidate's essay will demonstrate one or more of the following • it contains numerous errors in spelling/grammar/punctuation/sentence construction/paragraphing • knowledge and understanding of the text(s) are not used to answer the question • any analysis and evaluation attempted are unconvincing • the answer is simply too thin
Analysis of the text demonstrates:	• **thorough awareness** of the writer's techniques, through analysis, making **confident** use of critical terminology • **very detailed/thoughtful** explanation of stylistic devices supported by a **range of well-chosen** references and/or quotations	• **sound awareness** of the writer's techniques through analysis, making **good** use of critical terminology • **detailed explanation** of stylistic devices supported by **appropriate** references and/or quotation	• **an awareness** of the writer's techniques through analysis, making **some** use of critical terminology • explanation of stylistic devices supported by **some appropriate** references and/or quotation	• **some awareness of the more obvious** techniques used by the writer • **description of some** stylistic devices followed by limited reference and/or quotation	
Evaluation of the text is shown through:	• **a well developed** commentary of what has been enjoyed/gained from the text(s), supported by a **range** of well-chosen references to its relevant features	• **a reasonably developed** commentary of what has been enjoyed/gained from the text (s), supported by **appropriate** references to its relevant features	• **some** commentary of what has been enjoyed/gained from the text(s), supported by **some appropriate** references to its relevant features	• **brief** commentary of what has been enjoyed/gained from the text(s), followed by **brief** reference to its features	
The candidate:	• uses language to communicate a line of thought **very clearly** • uses spelling, grammar, sentence construction and punctuation which are **consistently** accurate • structures the essay **effectively to enhance** meaning/purpose • uses paragraphing which is **accurate and effective**	• uses language to communicate a line of thought **clearly** • uses spelling, grammar, sentence construction and punctuation which are **mainly** accurate • structures the essay **well** • uses paragraphing which is **accurate**	• uses language to communicate a line of thought **at first reading** • uses spelling, grammar, sentence construction and punctuation which are **sufficiently** accurate • attempts to structure the essay **in an appropriate way** • uses paragraphing which is sufficiently accurate	• uses language to communicate a line of thought which may be disorganised and/or difficult to follow • makes significant errors in spelling/grammar/sentence construction/punctuation • has not structured the essay well • has made significant errors in paragraphing	
In summary, the candidates essay is:	thorough and precise	very detailed and shows some insight	fairly detailed and relevant	lacks detail and relevance	superficial and/or technically weak

NATIONAL 5 ENGLISH
2016

READING FOR UNDERSTANDING, ANALYSIS AND EVALUATION

1. Any two points for 1 mark each.

   Glosses of:

   - "follow in the footsteps of Diana Ross and Whitney Houston" eg she was a great (female) singer/star too
   - "belt out" eg give a powerful delivery
   - "the voice of Elsa"/"the most successful animated film ..." eg she was the singer of the hit film/song
   - "ubiquitous" eg the song was heard everywhere (accept eg "was well known")
   - "Oscar-winning" eg the song was critically acclaimed
   - "more than three million copies sold" eg the song was (very) popular/profitable
   - "(more than passing) acquaintance" eg she has (good) experience "with anthems" eg of important/highly-regarded songs

2. 1 mark for reference; 1 mark for comment.
   - "stratospheric" eg suggests signal/immense/far-reaching/heightened achievement/out of this world
   - "(takings of more than) £800 million" OR "it's No 5 in the all-time list of highest-grossing films" OR uses statistics eg to show that the film has made a great deal of money
   - uses parenthesis to include (significant) statistics/evidence
   - "has elevated her" eg she has achieved greater prominence
   - "into a new league" eg into a different (superior) context

3. Any five points.

   Glosses of:

   - "she has clearly been reprimanded" eg they have a system of discipline/control
   - "by the Disney suits" eg they are conventionally dressed (ie reference to appearance)
   - "by the Disney suits" eg conservative/corporate/faceless (ie reference to attitude/mindset)
   - "Apparently I spoke out of turn" eg they disliked dissent
   - "Disney doesn't have sequels, (so it would be a first if there was one)" eg they don't (usually) produce follow-up films
   - "stage show" OR "six-minute short" OR "new song" indicates eg (commercial) versatility
   - "(much) mooted" eg Disney is the centre of speculation
   - "the Disney people keep things close to their chests" OR "tight-lipped" eg they are secretive/they say little
   - "happy to milk the commercial opportunities" OR "enjoyed a mighty bump" eg they take pleasure in exploiting/maximising the financial gain

4. 1 mark for reference; 1 mark for comment (×2).
   - "There to be shot at" eg suggests people's readiness to denigrate OR (image of) "shot at" illustrates eg the critics' aggression/hostility/targeting
   - "criticised" eg indicates open to negative comment
   - "failing to hit a high note" eg suggest harshness of criticism
   - parenthetical insertion (of "singing in sub-zero temperatures") eg serves to highlight the point
   - substance of "sub-zero temperatures" eg adverse conditions
   - "still some who noticed the odd flat note" eg suggests (excessive) vigilance of audience/inability to please everyone
   - "The unnerving" eg it is scary
   - "proximity" eg the footballers are close
   - "of several dozen" eg there are many of them
   - "hulking (American footballers)" OR "huge" eg they are very big/intimidating
   - "strong presence (these athletes have)" eg they have an aura/charisma
   - "you're this one woman, singing on her own" eg she was alone/an outnumbered female
   - "(they're so ...) daunting" eg (the men are) intimidating
   - use of ellipsis suggests she wants to be precise in her own comments/provides a dramatic pause/emphasises "daunting"

5. Any one pair OR two correct selections covering different directions.
   - "One woman" looks back to "one woman" OR "on her own" OR the idea of isolation
   - "squad of men" looks back to "several dozen hulking" OR "huge" OR "American footballers" OR the idea of male physical presence
   - "Frozen" looks forward to "Disney animation"
   - "a feminist breakthrough" looks forward to (idea of) "The first ... to be directed ... by a woman" OR "love ... between two sisters" OR "not because some Prince Charming is saving the day"
   - "One woman opposite a squad of men" (accept paraphrase) looks back to the isolation of Idina Menzel
   - information before colon looks back information after colon looks forward

6. 1 mark for reference; 1 mark for comment (×2).
   - "heroine" eg strength of character
   - "subtle" eg not straightforward
   - "conflicted" eg has contradictory emotions/internal battles/complications
   - "sorceress" eg supernatural
   - "struggling to control her powers" eg has difficulties with her abilities
   - "she keeps [Anna] at a distance" eg deliberately remote
   - "for fear of turning her into a popsicle" eg she wields (potentially harmful) power

- "(grandiose) sulks" eg is (spectacularly) moody
- "emo (princess)" eg alternative/sensitive/of dark mind or appearance/saturnine
- "(definitely) complicated" eg (undeniably) complex
- "not stereotypes" eg not predictable/what is conventionally expected

7. • her sister's company (beautifully) encapsulated key ideas of the films
   • **OR** Travolta's error heightened her profile
   • **OR** the song was up for (and won) an (top) award — "Oscar" may be lifted and she got to sing it

8. It is possible to gain full marks through examination of one linguistic aspect.

   Sentence structure:
   - long compared to short sentences **OR** appropriate contrasting references shows complexity compared simplicity

   Tone:
   - appropriate contrasting references eg "several zeitgeist-y things across different generations"/"people who are trying to find themselves" compared with "one more (burning) question"/"No I do not!" shows formality/seriousness compared to lightness/humour/vehemence

   Word choice:
   - "zeitgeist-y" **OR** "resonate" compared to "Does she have her own Elsa dress" shows the difference between difficulty and simplicity
   - "proud" and "much to learn" exhibits the difference between self-esteem and humility
   - "Rent to Wicked" **OR** "Glee to Frozen" illustrates then and now
   - "Frozen" and "burning". Comment must show understanding these are antonyms
   - "certainly aware" and "I have as much to learn myself". Comment must show understanding these are antonymous

9. *Any five from:*

Reference to	Glossed by (eg)
"I spoke out of turn"	She can be forthright/impulsive
"I'd have to play Elsa's mother, probably" or "she laughs"	She has a (self-deprecating) sense of humour
"she sounds slightly disappointed"	She likes to be the star/centre of attention/is self-centred
Despite criticisms	She shows persistence
"they're ... daunting"	She can be intimidated
"not because some Prince Charming is saving the day"	She is assertive/feminist (accept slang)
"It was Cara whom Menzel took as her date"	She is close to/fond of her sister/caring
"wincingly"	She is modest/embarrassed by her sister's admiration

Reference to	Glossed by (eg)
"she ... recognises ... Travolta's slip"	She is perceptive/realistic
"her conversation is a mix of Broadway-speak"	She can be/is shrewd enough to adapt to her environment/use platitudes
"battled-hardened"	She is tough/resilient
"ambition"	She has aspirations
"aware of the value of appearing"	She is shrewd/pragmatic
"I'm proud of that"	She relishes fans' identification with her
"I have as much to learn myself"	She is modest/self-aware
"I don't look that good as a blonde"	She is modest NB please don't credit 'modest' twice
"she'd also quite enjoy ruling over her own wintry kingdom"	She enjoys power/dominance/prominence

CRITICAL READING

SECTION 1 — SCOTTISH TEXT

PART A — DRAMA — *Bold Girls* by Rona Munro

1. Any three key points for 1 mark each.

   Candidates are expected to use their own words.

   Possible answers include:
   - Deirdre confronts Marie about the truth about Michael (her father)
   - Marie tries to avoid telling her the truth
   - Marie (loses her temper) and destroys the photograph of Michael
   - Marie sees Deirdre's bruises and asks about them
   - there is temporary physical closeness between the women
   - the women start to face up to the truth about Michael (and his affairs)
   - there is an increasing sense of understanding between the women by the end of the extract

2. 1 mark for reference; 1 mark for comment (×2).

   Possible answers include:
   - Marie is angry "Marie doesn't turn"
   - Marie is shocked "Marie turns startled"
   - Marie loses control of her emotions "... laugh hysterically"
   - Marie is frightened "Marie backs off a step"
   - Marie loses her temper "Suddenly Marie flies at her"

3. Candidates should make some of the following possible observations:
   - she destroys Michael's photograph which is surprising as it has been a symbol of her adulation/has dominated the setting/staging
   - she is aggressive in destroying the photograph which is surprising because she is usually calm
   - she immediately tidies up which is surprising because she seems to accept this as "closure"/returns to domestic role

4. Candidates should identify one attitude towards Marie (for 1 mark).

   Candidates should select a relevant piece of dialogue (for 1 mark) and explain fully how this conveys the attitude (for 1 mark).

   Possible answers include:

   - **Identification of attitude:** Deirdre is at points surprised/confused/upset/aggressive/calm/inquisitive

   - "But you'd know…" seeks the truth

   - "here, that's you got everything back" implies resentment

   - "I want the truth out of you. I mean it." short sentences gives emphatic tone/impatience/assertiveness

   - "Tell me!" exclamation/monosyllabic words indicate(s) impatience

   - "Just the fella she's got living with her just now." indicates she is accepting/philosophical about being a victim of domestic violence

5. Candidates should identify areas of conflict in the characters' lives from this scene and elsewhere in the play.

   Possible areas for comment include:

   - Marie and Deirdre seem to resolve their conflict as an understanding is reached between them by the end of the play.

   - Cassie and Nora's conflict grows as Cassie's plan to move away is revealed and she does not accept the truth about her father.

   - There is ongoing political conflict in the world beyond the immediate setting of the play.

   - There is conflict between the characters and their bleak setting. There are continued references to the blandness/drabness of the setting.

   - Conflict between men and women is a feature of the play. There are several examples of ongoing clashes between stereotypical male and female behaviour.

   - There is conflict between Cassie and Marie over the issue of infidelity.

   - Reference to the knife being a symbol of conflict.

   Candidates may choose to answer in **bullet points** in this final question, or write a number of linked statements. There is **no requirement** to write a "mini essay".

   Up to 2 marks can be achieved for identifying elements of commonality as requested in the question. A further 2 marks can be achieved for **reference to the extract given.**

   4 additional marks can be awarded for similar references to **at least one other part of the text.**

   <u>In practice this means:</u>

   Identification of commonality (eg theme, central relationship, importance of setting, use of imagery, development in characterisation, use of personal experience, use of dramatic devices or any other key element …)

   from the extract:

   1 relevant reference to technique; 1 appropriate comment

   OR 1 relevant reference to idea; 1 appropriate comment

   OR 1 relevant reference to feature; 1 appropriate comment

   OR 1 relevant reference to text; 1 appropriate comment

   (maximum of 2 marks only for discussion of extract)

   from **at least one other part of the text:**

   as above (×2) for **up to 4 marks**

PART A — DRAMA — *Sailmaker* by Alan Spence

6. Candidates should make four key points.

   Possible answers include:

   - Davie does not realise that Alec actually does need him/would like him to use his skills

   - Davie is already making excuses about not fixing up the yacht immediately

   - Davie indulges in unlawful gambling

   - Davie's lack of preparedness/homemaking skills

   - Does not provide financially for his family

   - asks Alec to go to the bookies for him against his will

7. For full marks candidates should identify two different aspects of Davie's mood, eg positive and negative, with supporting quotation/reference.

   Possible answers include:

   - **Lines 2–3:**

     Davie's mood is: sad, depressing, pessimistic, rejected, worthless, futile, angry etc (when discussing being made redundant as a sailmaker) "chucked"/"Nothin else doin"/"Nae work"/"Naebody needs sailmakers"

   - **Lines 10–16:**

     Davie's mood is optimistic, hopeful, humorous, excited, etc (when speaking about gambling) "wait an see"/"Who knows?"/"Maybe my coupon'll come up"/exaggerations about potential activity with winnings/"Never mind"/"Some ae these days"

8. (a) *Possible answers include:*

   - it is against the law to gamble

   - occasionally the bookmaker gets caught

   - gamblers protect their identity/avoid getting caught

   (b) Two clear points required for full marks (1 + 1).

   Possible answers include:

   - reveals he still considers himself a sailmaker pride/sense of identity/sense of importance

9. *Possible areas for comment include:*

   From the extract:

   - Alec gives Davie the yacht believing that he will fix it up represents his belief that Davie will live up to his promises.

   - Davie speaks knowledgably about the yacht revealing his past as a skilled worker.

   - Davie is already making excuses about why he can't fix up the yacht now.

   From elsewhere:

   - Alec speaks with admiration about his father's past as a Sailmaker to Ian, and believes that his dad will fix up the yacht for him to play with.

- Davie's continual lack of action in fixing the yacht represents his general procrastination in other matters/his bitterness at not being a Sailmaker/his prioritising (both in time and money) of gambling, drinking, etc.
- by contrast Billy paints the yacht immediately revealing that he is a different character who is proactive and keeps his word.
- Alec places the yacht in the Glory Hole when his dad loses his job as he realises this is not a good time for his dad to be reminded of it.
- Alec is accepting that his dad may not live up to his promises.
- in the final scene of the play the yacht is placed on the fire by Alec and Davie which shows an acceptance from Alec about the type of person/ father that Davie is.
- also represents the theme(s) of escape/childhood play, and relates to some of the music in the text, eg Red Sails in the Sunset, Will Your Anchor Hold, etc.

Candidates may choose to answer in **bullet points** in this final question, or write a number of linked statements. There is **no requirement** to write a "mini essay".

Up to 2 marks can be achieved for identifying elements of commonality as requested in the question. A further 2 marks can be achieved for **reference to the extract given.**

4 additional marks can be awarded for similar references to **at least one other part of the text.**

In practice this means:

Identification of commonality (eg theme, central relationship, importance of setting, use of imagery, development in characterisation, use of personal experience, use of dramatic devices or any other key element...)

from the extract:

1 relevant reference to technique; 1 appropriate comment

OR 1 relevant reference to idea; 1 appropriate comment

OR 1 relevant reference to feature; 1 appropriate comment

OR 1 relevant reference to text; 1 appropriate comment

(maximum of 2 marks only for discussion of extract)

from **at least one other part of the text:**

as above (×2) for **up to 4 marks**

PART A — DRAMA — *Tally's Blood* by Ann Marie Di Mambro

10. Candidates should make four key points for 1 mark each.

    Any four points.

    Possible answers include:

    - Bridget accuses Rosinella of making Lucia leave
    - Rosinella is confused about why Bridget is angry
    - Bridget accuses Rosinella of interfering in her relationship with Franco by making her feel that it wasn't genuine
    - Rosinella denies Bridget's accusations
    - Rosinella is annoyed that Bridget mentions Franco or their relationship
    - Rosinella expresses how upset she is that Lucia has left because of how much she loves her

    - Rosinella admits that she is glad that Lucia and Hughie will not be together
    - Rosinella wants to pretend this argument did not happen
    - Bridget reveals that she was pregnant with Franco's child

11. Candidates should deal with both word choice and sentence structure – 2 marks are available for each.

    1 mark for reference; 1 mark for comment (×2).

    Possible answers include:

    Word choice:

    - "you made me" eg suggests she is resentful of Rosinella's interference
    - "nothing (to him)" eg sense of worthlessness
    - "just a wee" eg sense of insignificance
    - "Scottish tart" eg lacking in importance or virtue
    - "no a day goes past..." eg lasting impact/inescapable aspect
    - "Franco loved me" eg simplistic but bold statement

    Sentence structure:

    - use of/repetition of (Rosinella's) question eg to suggest her outrage
    - repeated "you" eg creating an accusatory tone
    - use of dash eg to suggest that Rosinella treated Bridget like an afterthought
    - short clipped sentence eg to show she powerfully disagrees with Rosinella
    - repetition of "Franco loved me." eg to suggest emphatic nature of her belief

12. Candidates should identify two different attitudes with a supporting reference for each attitude.

    1 mark for reference; 1 mark for comment (×2).

    Possible answers include:

    - confused eg use of questions/repeating Bridget's words
    - defensive eg "What did I ever do to you?"
    - annoyed eg "Angry"
    - rude eg calls Bridget "lady"
    - contemptuous eg "Dismissive"
    - trivialising eg "What you going on about now?"
    - shocked eg "shakes her head"/"backs off in disbelief"

13. *Possible areas for comment include:*

    From the extract:

    - family willing to defend each other eg Bridget taking on Rosinella for Hughie
    - family looking out for each other eg Rosinella and Massimo looking after Lucia even though she is not their child
    - family interfering in romantic relationships eg Rosinella disapproving of Hughie and Lucia as well as Bridget and Franco

From elsewhere:

- conflict eg family arguments about children not doing as expected by their parents or family (Massimo opening his own shop/Franco joining the army)
- love/loyalty: characters looking after family members eg Rosinella and her father in law, Bridget and Hughie with their mother and siblings, Rosinella and Massimo with Lucia

Candidates may choose to answer in **bullet points** in this final question, or write a number of linked statements. There is **no requirement** to write a "mini essay".

Up to 2 marks can be achieved for identifying elements of commonality as requested in the question. A further 2 marks can be achieved for **reference to the extract given.**

4 additional marks can be awarded for similar references to **at least one other part of the text.**

In practice this means:

Identification of commonality (eg theme, central relationship, importance of setting, use of imagery, development in characterisation, use of personal experience, use of dramatic devices or any other key element...)

from the extract:

1 relevant reference to technique; 1 appropriate comment

OR 1 relevant reference to idea; 1 appropriate comment

OR 1 relevant reference to feature; 1 appropriate comment

OR 1 relevant reference to text; 1 appropriate comment

(maximum of 2 marks only for discussion of extract)

from **at least one other part of the text:**

as above (×2) for **up to 4 marks**

PART B — PROSE — *The Cone-Gatherers* by Robin Jenkins

14. Candidates should explain how the writer uses two examples of language to effectively describe Roderick's imaginings.

Reference should be made to lines 1–9.

1 mark for reference; 1 mark for comment (×2).

Possible answers include:

Word choice:

- "yew" has connotations of/links with death/Roderick imagines the cone-gatherers dead/murdered
- "stalking" describes Duror's walk as predatory
- "gloat" describes Duror's sense of smug satisfaction

Contrast:

- the reference to "tall"/"frowned" and "small"/"smiled" to illustrate the differences in the two men

Sound:

- (onomatopoeia of) "cracked" suggests the loud/clear/frightening sound of the gunfire

Imagery:

- "idea took root" links with trees and suggests the thought forming/developing in Roderick's mind
- "green bony arms" personifies the branches and suggests care/support

Sentence structure:

- short sentence "That idea sprouted" adds impact due to its brevity. Suggests the importance of Roderick's thoughts

15. Candidates should explain two different ways in which Roderick thinks of death in lines 10–19.

Candidates should use their own words as far as possible.

Possible answers include:

- "distant death was commonplace" — Roderick thinks of death as far away and/or a normal/regular occurrence
- "loyally been pleased" — Roderick thinks it is honourable/death of enemy is a good thing/he is patriotic
- "death ... as a tyrant" — Roderick thought of death as cruel when it took someone he loved (his grandfather)/personally affected him
- imagines the death of Duror as a sense of despair/damage/hopelessness...

16. Candidates should explain how the writer uses two examples of language to create a frightening atmosphere in lines 17–24.

1 mark for reference; 1 mark for comment (×2).

Possible answers include:

- reference to "desolation" suggests world completely barren
- reference to (every single leaf was) polluted suggests toxic atmosphere etc
- image of deaths gathering to seek revenge suggests that Roderick fears his earlier loyalty/patriotism was wrong
- question (about the death of evil and triumph of good) suggests that Roderick is unsure of the power of goodness
- atmosphere of darkness and silence, created by lack of sun and birdsong suggests an eerie quiet/the calm before the storm
- reference to the "hut in shadow" is typical of the horror genre/suggests evil to follow
- Roderick is too frightened to either cry or pray suggests he is overcome by the power of evil in the wood

17. 1 mark for reference; 1 mark for comment (×2).

Possible answers include:

- "Without any interpretable gesture" suggests his actions are hard to understand/confusing
- "without a sound" suggests stealth/sinister movements
- "(turned and) vanished" suggests sudden/magical disappearance
- "(as if this time) forever" suggests finality

18. Candidates should discuss why war is an important feature in this extract and elsewhere in the novel.

Possible areas for comment include:

- The setting of war is important as it places the characters in the wood at the same time: the brothers to gather cones, Duror to manage the estate and Lady Runcie-Campbell in charge in the absence of Sir Colin.

- **OR** the war reflects the conflict within and between a number of characters – eg within Duror/between him and the cone-gatherers/Roderick and the class system …

From the extract:

- Roderick is reminded of the war and its many deaths which he had initially greeted with patriotic loyalty

- **OR** the news of deaths heard on the radio is a regular feature and influences Roderick's thoughts of death in the woods, adding to his fears

From elsewhere:

- initial description of setting — idyllic with the subtle reference to the destroyer

- Duror is at war with himself — acknowledged on many occasions throughout the novel, often by references to sick/dying trees

- Duror's frustration at being too old to enlist partly fuels his hatred of the cone-gatherers

- Duror's wish to eliminate the cone-gatherers from the wood is linked to his sympathies for Hitler's actions against the Jews

- the war has allowed Duror to have the power that he has on the estate: Sir Colin is absent and Lady Runcie-Campbell relies on him for advice on estate management

- the wood is a microcosm of the world at war — Duror is waging his own war on the cone-gatherers whom he sees as inferior and should be eliminated; his own death at the end can be likened to Hitler's suicide

Candidates may choose to answer in **bullet points** in this final question, or write a number of linked statements. There is **no requirement** to write a "mini essay".

Up to 2 marks can be achieved for identifying elements of commonality as requested in the question. A further 2 marks can be achieved for **reference to the extract given.**

4 additional marks can be awarded for similar references to **at least one other part of the text.**

In practice this means:

Identification of commonality (eg theme, central relationship, importance of setting, use of imagery, development in characterisation, use of personal experience, use of dramatic devices or any other key element…)

from the extract:

1 relevant reference to technique; 1 appropriate comment

OR 1 relevant reference to idea; 1 appropriate comment

OR 1 relevant reference to feature; 1 appropriate comment

OR 1 relevant reference to text; 1 appropriate comment

(maximum of 2 marks only for discussion of extract)

from **at least one other part of the text:**

as above (×2) for **up to 4 marks**

PART B — PROSE — *The Testament of Gideon Mack* **by James Robertson**

19. Four relevant points for 1 mark each.

    Candidates should use their own words as far as possible.

Possible answers include:

- Mack is discovered alive and with no serious injury his speedy recovery surprises doctors

- he doesn't seem keen to start back at his job

- he tells people about his ordeal and says he met the Devil who rescued him

- people think he has gone mad or similar and some are cross that he is saying things which are unchristian

- Mack takes the funeral of a friend but this is controversial as he speaks of meeting the Devil here too

- he is reported to the Presbytery

- there is a sort of a trial and Mack admits to what he has done but doesn't see anything wrong in it

- he is suspended until the main trial can take place but before that can happen Mack disappears

20. 1 mark for reference; 1 mark for comment (×2).

Possible answers include:

- "apparently" suggests it is not certain

- "(even more) amazingly" **OR** reference to parenthesis suggests incredulity

- "somehow" suggests near impossibility

- "no creature … survive" suggests he should not have lived through it

- "astonished" suggests no-one can believe it

21. 1 mark for reference; 1 mark for comment (×2).

Possible answers include:

- "no great hurry … duties" suggests lazy/distracted

- "claimed"/"improbable"/"unorthodox"/reference to the unlikely story suggests madness or delusions

- "assert"/"insisted" suggests he is convinced of it/sure of himself/strength of character

- "frailty" suggests weakness

- "irreverent"/"scandalous"/"incompatible … minister"/"no option but to refer" suggests he is offensive/blasphemous

22. *Possible areas for comment include:*

- Candidates should identify one theme introduced in this extract and discuss how it is explored elsewhere in the novel.

Possible themes include:

- truth

- religion

- the supernatural

- stories within stories

- madness

- belief

Candidates may choose to answer in **bullet points** in this final question, or write a number of linked statements. There is **no requirement** to write a "mini essay".

Up to 2 marks can be achieved for identifying elements of commonality as requested in the question. A further 2 marks can be achieved for **reference to the extract given.**

4 additional marks can be awarded for similar references to **at least one other part of the text.**

In practice this means:

Identification of commonality (eg theme, central relationship, importance of setting, use of imagery, development in characterisation, use of personal experience, use of dramatic devices or any other key element...)

from the extract:

1 relevant reference to technique; 1 appropriate comment

OR 1 relevant reference to idea; 1 appropriate comment

OR 1 relevant reference to feature; 1 appropriate comment

OR 1 relevant reference to text; 1 appropriate comment

(maximum of 2 marks only for discussion of extract)

from **at least one other part of the text:**

as above (×2) for **up to 4 marks**

PART B — PROSE — *Kidnapped* **by Robert Louis Stevenson**

23. 1 mark for reference; 1 mark for comment (×2).

    Possible answers include:

    • "it was so dark inside"/"in the pitch darkness" suggests going into the unknown

    • "a body could scarce breathe" holding breath due to fear

    • "with a beating heart" infers heart beating fast due to danger

    • "Minding my uncle's word about the banisters" infers thinking about warning (outlined by his uncle)

    • "I pushed out with foot and hand" proceeded carefully due to fear

    • "by the touch" indicates caution as he feels his way in the dark

    • "felt my way" indicates caution as he feels his way in the dark

24. 1 mark for realisation; 1 mark for mood.

    Possible answers include:

    Realisation:

    • Ebenezer has tried to kill David by sending him to the tower

    Mood:

    • David feels furious/David wishes to gain some revenge for his uncle's actions/David is determined to get revenge even if it causes him harm in the process/David feels some bravery at the realisation

25. *Possible answers include:*

    • David reaches the top of the stairs

    • David realises there is nothing there

    • he discovers that the staircase ends suddenly

    • he realises he is in great danger/he could have died

    • he is physically affected by fear

    • he starts to make his way down

    • his downward journey is full of anger

    • the storm rises

    • he sees a light in the kitchen

    • he sees his uncle

    • there is loud thunder

26. 1 mark for reference; 1 mark for comment.

    Possible answers include:

    • "wind sprang up" emphasises the suddenness and speed that the wind appears

    • "clap" emphasises the physical power and suddenness of the wind

    • "died (again)" emphasises the speed that the wind disappeared

    • "it fell in buckets" the volume of rain is emphasised in that it seemed to be torrential

    • "blinding flash" the intensity of the lightning is emphasised

    • "tow-row" emphasises the very noisy nature of the thunder

27. *Possible areas for comment include:*

    • David's kidnapping

    • the roundhouse scene on the Covenant

    • the murder of Red Fox

    • the escape across the heather

    • the tension after the card game at Cluny's Cage

    • any of the many moments of tension between David and Alan throughout the novel

    • the confrontation with Ebenezer at the end of the novel

    Candidates may choose to answer in **bullet points** in this final question, or write a number of linked statements. There is **no requirement** to write a "mini essay".

    Up to 2 marks can be achieved for identifying elements of commonality as requested in the question. A further 2 marks can be achieved for **reference to the extract given.**

    4 additional marks can be awarded for similar references to **at least one other part of the text.**

    In practice this means:

    Identification of commonality (eg theme, central relationship, importance of setting, use of imagery, development in characterisation, use of personal experience, use of dramatic devices or any other key element...)

    from the extract:

    1 relevant reference to technique; 1 appropriate comment

    OR 1 relevant reference to idea; 1 appropriate comment

    OR 1 relevant reference to feature; 1 appropriate comment

    OR 1 relevant reference to text; 1 appropriate comment

    (maximum of 2 marks only for discussion of extract)

    from **at least one other part of the text:**

    as above (×2) for **up to 4 marks**

PART B — PROSE — *The Painter* **by Iain Crichton Smith**

28. 1 mark for reference; 1 mark for comment.

    Possible answers include:

    • "sitting comfortably"

      relaxed/at ease/calm

    • "no expression"

      impassive/detached/disengaged

- "cold clear intensity"/reference to alliteration indifferent/focused/unresponsive

29. 1 mark for reference; 1 mark for comment (×2).

Possible answers include:

- "scythes" is a dangerous implement
- "swing" highlights dangerous nature of weapons/how they were being used
- "contorted" suggests intensity/strength of their anger distorts their faces
- "fury" suggests fierce/angry nature of the encounter
- "(of) battle" suggests a fierce/powerful/hostile encounter
- "suffused" suggests full of/consumed/visibly roused
- "blood" suggests violence/harm
- "(and) rage" suggests intense/deep-rooted/ passionate hatred for each other
- Repetition of "as" conveys the energy/tension/ physical nature of the fight
- "teeth drawn … snarl" suggests animal-like brutality

30. *Possible answers include:*

"admiration"

- his ability to remain focused on his work
- the depth/single-mindedness of his focus
- his disregard for his own safety

"bitter disgust"

- his detachment/isolation from the villagers ("gaze … beyond the human")
- his impartial/unemotional stance
- his coldness/superiority to those around him (comparison to hawk)
- his reaction to the disruption to his painting ("blind fury")
- his visible emotion relating to the conflict ("tears of rage"/"still snarling")
- his departure from the conflict with the narrator

31. *Possible answers include:*

- he is ignored
- they are troubled by him/they don't understand him
- he is seen as being different/an outsider
- he is rejected
- his work is destroyed
- he does not conform with their code of conduct

32. *Possible areas for comment include:*

- **"The Telegram"** — the "thin woman's" reputation as an outsider due to the sacrifices she has made for her son
- **"The Red Door"** — Murdo's discontent leading to his desire to be independent from the constraints of village life; Mary's independence shown by her choice of clothing/creativity etc.
- **"Mother and Son"** — John's isolation from his peers/ lack of confidence due to his mother's constant criticism/control/dominance

- **"In Church"** — "The priest" (a deserter who is in hiding) is at odds with society, having lost all sense of humanity
- **"The Crater"** — Robert feels at odds with his role as an Officer in a war time situation

Candidates may choose to answer in **bullet points** in this final question, or write a number of linked statements. There is **no requirement** to write a "mini essay".

Up to 2 marks can be achieved for identifying elements of commonality as requested in the question. A further 2 marks can be achieved for **reference to the extract given**.

4 additional marks can be awarded for similar references to **at least one other part of the text**.

<u>In practice this means:</u>

Identification of commonality (eg theme, central relationship, importance of setting, use of imagery, development in characterisation, use of personal experience, use of dramatic devices or any other key element…)

from the extract:

1 relevant reference to technique; 1 appropriate comment

OR 1 relevant reference to idea; 1 appropriate comment

OR 1 relevant reference to feature; 1 appropriate comment

OR 1 relevant reference to text; 1 appropriate comment

(maximum of 2 marks only for discussion of extract)

from **at least one other part of the text:**

as above (×2) for **up to 4 marks**

PART B — PROSE — *Dear Santa* by Anne Donovan

33. Four points for 1 mark each.

Possible answers include:

- Alison is writing a letter to Santa
- she is trying to ask him to make her mother love her
- she is finding writing the letter difficult
- she doesn't believe Santa can make her mother love her
- she isn't sure if she believes in Santa
- she is feeling unhappy/pessimistic
- her mother comes into the bedroom/looks after Katie/spends time with Alison
- Alison finishes the letter but does not ask for what she really wants
- Alison and her mother spend some close/loving time together
- Alison demonstrates her affection for her mother
- Alison's mother demonstrates a little affection towards Alison
- at the end of the extract it is suggested there is hope for their relationship

34. 1 mark for reference; 1 mark for comment.

Possible answers include:

- "the page ah'm starin at" suggests it is hard for her to start the letter
- "it's hard tae find the words" shows she finds it difficult to say what she really wants/feels

- unfinished sentences emphasise how hard she finds it to put her feelings into words
- repeated questions suggest she doubts her request would work
- negative answers reinforce the fact that she doubts whether a letter to Santa would be effective
- reference to grey outside/no white Christmas reflects the negativity of her mood
- the fact that she doesn't write down what she actually wants shows she doesn't think it's achievable

35. (a) 1 mark for reference; 1 mark for comment.

Possible answers include:

- "Hair glowin like a halo" — suggests angelic, connotations of goodness, bringing light into darkness, positivity, etc
- (hair) "soft and fuzzy" — makes the mother seem kind and gentle
- "she's in a good mood" etc, suggests she's mellowed towards Alison and is allowing her to be closer
- "There's nothing wrang wi broon hair" suggests she understands Alison wants to be more like her and Katie but she reassures her that she is fine the way she is
- "She looks at me mair soft like" — suggests more loving
- "She kisses me" — suggests affection
- "nearly", or reference to "a wee crack of light" suggests hope that the relationship can be rebuilt/ that there is some love there

(b) 1 mark for reference; 1 mark for comment.

Possible answers showing negative contrast include:

- "she cannae be bothered wi that"/"jerks her heid away"/"sayin don't"/"you'll mess it up" suggests mother doesn't like physical contact with Alison
- "dry (kiss)" suggests limited, grudging, etc
- "barely grazing" suggests mother hasn't much time for Alison
- "before ah've kissed her back" suggests she does not really want physical contact with Alison
- "closin the door" suggests putting up a barrier between herself and Alison, or similar

36. *Possible areas for comment include:*

- **"Virtual Pals"** — Siobhan's lack of confidence; boyfriend issues; growing up; relationships
- **"Zimmerobics"** — old age and associated problems; loneliness
- **"All that Glisters"** — how Clare copes with her father's illness and death; how she copes with difficult adults such as the shopkeeper and her aunt; how she overcomes challenges; how she supports her mother in her grief; how she celebrates her daddy
- **"A Chitterin Bite"** — relationships; lack of confidence; inability to move on; as a child, Mary does not deal well with Agnes growing up and moving on; as an adult, she resolves her personal difficulties by taking control and ending the affair

Candidates may choose to answer in **bullet points** in this final question, or write a number of linked statements. There is **no requirement** to write a "mini essay".

Up to 2 marks can be achieved for identifying elements of commonality as requested in the question. A further 2 marks can be achieved for **reference to the extract given**.

4 additional marks can be awarded for similar references to **at least one other part of the text.**

In practice this means:

Identification of commonality (eg theme, central relationship, importance of setting, use of imagery, development in characterisation, use of personal experience, use of dramatic devices or any other key element...)

from the extract:

1 relevant reference to technique; 1 appropriate comment

OR 1 relevant reference to idea; 1 appropriate comment

OR 1 relevant reference to feature; 1 appropriate comment

OR 1 relevant reference to text; 1 appropriate comment

(maximum of 2 marks only for discussion of extract)

from **at least one other part of the text:**

as above (×2) for **up to 4 marks**

PART C — POETRY — *Originally* **by Carol Ann Duffy**

37. 1 mark for each point made. Candidates must use their own words.

Possible answers include:

- gloss of "red room" — reference to vehicle
- gloss of "fell" — travelled downhill/in a downwards direction
- gloss of "through the fields" — travelled through the country/countryside
- gloss of "mother singing" — reference to her mother's voice
- gloss of "My brothers cried"/"bawling" — brothers being upset
- gloss of "miles rushed back ... etc" — sense of leaving somewhere/distance
- gloss of "toy ... holding its paw, etc" — had comfort of toy/teddy

38. 1 mark for reference; 1 mark for comment (×2).

Possible answers include:

- "slow" a gradual awareness of the new surroundings/a gradual build-up of feelings in response to the move
- "leaving you standing" you find yourself isolated
- "resigned" you have to accept things/learn to accept things
- "up an avenue" you can be lonely
- "sudden" change can seem quick/unexpected
- "Your accent wrong" you feel out of place/don't fit in
- "unimagined" you haven't been able to picture new surroundings

- "pebble-dashed estates" find yourself in unfamiliar surroundings
- "big boys eating worms" people seem very different
- "shouting words you don't understand" language barriers
- "parents' anxiety" you sense other people's worries
- "stirred like a loose tooth" you become aware that things are different
- "I want our own country" you miss your old surroundings/want to return

39. 1 mark for reference; 1 mark for comment (×2).

Possible answers include:

- "But" suggests a change from being an outsider to accepting her new surroundings
- "then you forget/don't recall" suggests your memory blots out old life
- "change" you adapt to your surroundings
- "brother swallow a slug" suggests awareness that other family members are accepting the local culture
- "skelf of shame" suggests how little guilt is felt in accepting the local culture
- "my tongue ... snake" suggests a casting off of old life, just as a snake casts off its old skin
- "my voice ... like the rest" suggests she's fitting in with the local culture

40. 1 mark for reference; 1 mark for comment.

Possible answers include:

- the use of the title "Originally" rounds off/brings a sense of closure
- the use of "Originally" links back to the discussion of where you come from/your origins (an important theme of the poem)
- "hesitates" suggests uncertainty about national/cultural identity (one of the main themes of the poem)/suggests acceptance of new surroundings

41. *Possible areas for comment include:*

- **"Originally"** — memory, identity/sense of belonging/acceptance/isolation, etc
- **"War Photographer"** — memory, painful memories, human cruelty, etc
- **"Valentine"** — different aspects of love, relationships, etc
- **"Havisham"** — jealousy/hard heartedness, rejection, etc
- **"Anne Hathaway"** — love, relationships, etc
- **"Mrs Midas"** — love, relationships, change, etc

Other answers are possible.

Candidates may choose to answer in **bullet points** in this final question, or write a number of linked statements. There is **no requirement** to write a "mini essay".

Up to 2 marks can be achieved for identifying elements of commonality as requested in the question. A further 2 marks can be achieved for **reference to the extract given**.

4 additional marks can be awarded for similar references to **at least one other part of the text**.

In practice this means:

Identification of commonality (eg theme, central relationship, importance of setting, use of imagery, development in characterisation, use of personal experience, use of dramatic devices or any other key element...)

from the extract:

1 relevant reference to technique; 1 appropriate comment

OR 1 relevant reference to idea; 1 appropriate comment

OR 1 relevant reference to feature; 1 appropriate comment

OR 1 relevant reference to text; 1 appropriate comment

(maximum of 2 marks only for discussion of extract)

from **at least one other part of the text:**

as above (×2) for **up to 4 marks**

PART C — POETRY — *Good Friday* **by Edwin Morgan**

42. Two references plus comments on what we learn about the drunken man.

1 mark for reference; 1 mark for comment (×2).

Possible answers include:

- "D's this go"/"right along Bath Street?" shows that he's confused
- "I've got to get some Easter eggs for the kiddies" shows he is kind/generous
- "I don't say it's right" **OR** "I'm no saying it's right" shows he is aware that his drinking on a religious holiday could be disagreed with
- "ye understand — ye understand?" shows that he wants the poet to empathise/doesn't want to be judged harshly
- "I'm no boring you, eh?" shows his desire to be listened to/accepted

43. (a) 1 mark for reference; 1 mark for comment.

Possible answers include:

- use of Glaswegian dialect suggests sense of place
- use of second person suggests the man is speaking directly to someone else
- use of long winding sentences suggests the man is rambling
- use of dashes/pauses suggests hesitation/loss of train of thought
- use of questions suggests he's seeking agreement
- use of repetition suggests immediacy of speech

(b) 1 mark for reference; 1 mark for identification of idea or concern (×2).

Possible answers include:

- "take today, I don't know what today's in aid of" suggests eg (religious) ignorance
- "whether Christ was — crucified or was he–" suggests eg religious doubt/ignorance
- "You're an educatit man, you can tell me" suggests eg awareness of class/educational differences
- "the working man has nae education" suggests eg awareness of lack of opportunities
- "he's just bliddy ignorant" suggests eg awareness/acceptance of lack of education

44. For 2 marks, candidates should refer to a feature of the last five lines and how it effectively continues an idea/language feature from earlier in the poem.

Possible answers include:

- "The bus brakes violently" echoes the opening lines which focus on the bus's movements
- "He lunges for the stair, swings down – off" echoes the opening lines which focus on the drunken man's movements
- "for his Easter eggs" recalls the drunk man's task/setting in time/title
- the structure of the last few lines

   OR

   "on very

      nearly

         steady

            legs"

   emphasises the man's drunkenness

45. *Possible comments on other poems:*

- **"Good Friday"** – religion, compassion, class in terms of education
- **"Trio"** – supernatural, passing of time, alienation, religion
- **"Slate"** – change, ie making a fresh start (politically or personally), change over time, adapting to change, identity, hopeful
- **"Hyena"** – death, brutality, survival, isolation, fear, perseverance of the hunter, alienation through fear, suffering
- **"In the Snack Bar"** – determination, compassion, isolation, perseverance, alienation, helplessness, suffering
- **"Winter"** – death and the relentless passing of time, progress of time, aging, suffering

Candidates may choose to answer in **bullet points** in this final question, or write a number of linked statements. There is **no requirement** to write a "mini essay".

Up to 2 marks can be achieved for identifying elements of commonality as requested in the question. A further 2 marks can be achieved for **reference to the extract given.**

4 additional marks can be awarded for similar references to **at least one other part of the text.**

In practice this means:

Identification of commonality (eg theme, central relationship, importance of setting, use of imagery, development in characterisation, use of personal experience, use of dramatic devices or any other key element...)

from the extract:

1 relevant reference to technique; 1 appropriate comment

OR 1 relevant reference to idea; 1 appropriate comment

OR 1 relevant reference to feature; 1 appropriate comment

OR 1 relevant reference to text; 1 appropriate comment

(maximum of 2 marks only for discussion of extract)

from **at least one other part of the text:**

as above (×2) for **up to 4 marks**

PART C — POETRY — *Sounds of the Day* **by Norman MacCaig**

46. Two points for 2 marks.

Possible answers include:

- he seems unconcerned/untroubled by them
- he seems comforted by them
- he reacts to them in a positive way
- they are familiar to him

47. 1 mark for reference; 1 mark for comment.

Possible answers include:

- "clatter" is a harsh/unsettling sound
- "creak" is an eerie sound/suggestive of the "door scraped shut" (which is to follow in line 10)
- "snuffling" suggests crying
- "puff" suggests something sudden
- "seeing us off" suggests aggression/parting
- "blocking ... unblocking" lack of constancy/ever changing
- "black drums rolled" suggests portent/sign of trouble
- "falling" suggests doom/troubling consequences

48. 1 mark for reference; 1 mark for comment (×2).

Possible answers include:

- "(door) scraped (shut)" harsh sound/contrasting sound with earlier (relative) calm
- "shut" is final/ominous
- "(the) end" suggests closed off/cut off/finality
- "all the sounds" suggests an all-encompassing change
- "you (left me)" contrast with "us" from verse 1/sense of separation
- "left me" suggests isolation/loneliness/upset
- "quietest fire" suggests silence/is opposite of earlier normal sounds/oxymoron/paradox/superlative

49. 1 mark for reference; 1 mark for comment (×2).

Possible answers include:

- "I thought" suggests poet's uncertainty
- "hurt in my pride only" suggests initial limited impact
- "forgetting that" suggests impact was not immediate
- "plunge" impact was deep
- "freezing (water)" suggests cold/unpleasant effects
- "ice" suggests extreme coldness of feeling
- identification of image of "bangle of ice" image suggests memories/burden of memory/weight of memory
- "whole" suggests completeness of effect
- "numb" suggests he has been overwhelmed, etc

50. *Possible areas for comment include:*

- **"Assisi"** – feelings of anger, outrage, bitterness
- **"Aunt Julia"** – feelings of nostalgia, loss, confusion, etc
- **"Basking Shark"** – feelings of confusion, doubt, shock, etc
- **"Visiting Hour"** – feelings of sadness, loss, unworthiness, etc
- **"Memorial"** – sadness, loss, etc

Candidates may choose to answer in **bullet points** in this final question, or write a number of linked statements. There is **no requirement** to write a "mini essay".

Up to 2 marks can be achieved for identifying elements of commonality as requested in the question. A further 2 marks can be achieved for **reference to the extract given.**

4 additional marks can be awarded for similar references to **at least one other part of the text.**

In practice this means:

Identification of commonality (eg theme, central relationship, importance of setting, use of imagery, development in characterisation, use of personal experience, use of dramatic devices or any other key element...)

from the extract:

1 relevant reference to technique; 1 appropriate comment

OR 1 relevant reference to idea; 1 appropriate comment

OR 1 relevant reference to feature; 1 appropriate comment

OR 1 relevant reference to text; 1 appropriate comment

(maximum of 2 marks only for discussion of extract)

from **at least one other part of the text:**

as above (×2) for **up to 4 marks**

PART C — POETRY — *Keeping Orchids* by Jackie Kay

51. Candidates must use their own words as far as possible.

    1 mark for a valid answer (×2).

    Possible answers include:

    - the (first person) narrator describes what happens when she meets her mother for the first time
    - there is an awkward atmosphere between the two women
    - the mother gives the narrator flowers (orchids)
    - orchids are rare/exotic and (therefore) difficult to look after/this symbolises the precarious nature of their relationship
    - the vase of flowers spills twice /symbolises the fragile nature of their relationship
    - the narrator tries to sort out the flower arrangement but she is not good at it/symbolises her feelings of awkwardness
    - some of the buds stay shut
    - the narrator sees the flowers as a burden/ responsibility (not a pleasure)

52. **Word choice:** 1 mark for reference; 1 mark for comment.

    Structure: 1 mark for reference; 1 mark for comment.

    Possible answers of word choice include:

    - "first (met)" establishes the importance of that moment
    - "twelve days later" shows how much time has elapsed since the meeting
    - "Twice since" shows the effort put in to take the flowers home
    - "Even after that" shows that time seems to be against the flowers

    - repetition of "twelve days later" reiterates the distance since the meeting time
    - "fading fast" suggests the haziness of time passing

    Possible answers on structure include:

    - the poem is written in couplets which gives a regular (predictable) pace/rhythm to indicate time passing steadily
    - there is repeated use of enjambment to indicate the pace of events
    - the frequent use of conjunctives moves the story of the poem forward at a fast pace
    - parenthesis is limited indicating the urgency to recount only the basic account of what happened
    - short sentences indicate the poet's intention to summarise events as succinctly as possible
    - repetition of "twice since" reiterates frequency of an event

53. 1 mark for reference; 1 mark for comment (x3).

    Possible answers include:

    - "voice rushes through a tunnel the other way" suggests distance
    - "try to remember" shows lack of clarity/shows the physical distance
    - "a paisley pattern scarf, a brooch" suggests the mother is dressed up for the occasion
    - "her hands, awkward and hard to hold" suggests lack of familiarity of touch
    - "fold and unfold" suggests the mother is fidgeting
    - "the story of her life" suggests lack of familiarity
    - "Compressed" suggests stiffness/only revealing the bare minimum of details
    - "Airtight" suggests defensiveness/being impenetrable

54. *Possible areas for comment include:*

    - the difference between appearance and reality
    - the conflict within family relationships
    - the difficulties of parenthood
    - the changing roles we perform as family members
    - the influence of time in shaping our memories/point of view
    - the importance of setting in shaping our behaviour/ influencing our thinking
    - the complex nature of love
    - the acceptance of imperfection
    - the development of self-awareness through time
    - the complexities of degeneration/decay

    Candidates may choose to answer in **bullet points** in this final question, or write a number of linked statements. There is **no requirement** to write a "mini essay".

    Up to 2 marks can be achieved for identifying elements of commonality as requested in the question. A further 2 marks can be achieved for **reference to the extract given.**

    4 additional marks can be awarded for similar references to **at least one other part of the text.**

<u>In practice this means:</u>

Identification of commonality (eg theme, central relationship, importance of setting, use of imagery, development in characterisation, use of personal experience, use of dramatic devices or any other key element...)

from the extract:

1 relevant reference to technique; 1 appropriate comment

OR 1 relevant reference to idea; 1 appropriate comment

OR 1 relevant reference to feature; 1 appropriate comment

OR 1 relevant reference to text; 1 appropriate comment

(maximum of 2 marks only for discussion of extract)

from **at least one other part of the text:**

as above (×2) for **up to 4 marks**

SECTION 2 — CRITICAL ESSAY

Please see the assessment criteria for the Critical Essay on page 130.

NATIONAL 5 ENGLISH 2017

READING FOR UNDERSTANDING, ANALYSIS AND EVALUATION

1. 1 mark for any one reference; 1 mark for comment.

    Possible answers include:

    - "We played ... every afternoon" suggests e.g. that it was their major pastime
    - "Sometimes other kids would join us" suggests e.g. occasionally they had more friends/bigger game/community
    - "in the summer we never seemed to leave"/"game after game"/"sometimes until it got dark" suggests e.g. that they played constantly/all day
    - "endlessly" suggests e.g. enjoyment seemed never to stop
    - "absorbing" suggests e.g. that they found it fascinating/fulfilling/all-consuming
    - "dim glow of street lights" suggests e.g. nostalgia
    - "two litre bottle of orange squash" suggests e.g. simple childhood pleasures/nostalgia
    - "pass it from player to player" suggests e.g. camaraderie/innocence
    - "none of us deterred by [warmth]" suggests e.g. nothing would put them off
    - "it tasted good" suggests e.g. that the experience was pleasurable
      NB "good" on its own not sufficient.

2. Any four points.

    Glosses of:

    - "never made it onto the school team" e.g. was never picked/selected
      NB "team" need not be glossed
    - "He kept trying"/"kept going to the trials"/"both at primary and senior school" e.g. persevered with opportunities for selection
    - "he was just off the pace" e.g. he was not quite fast/skilled enough
    - "He yearned to play" e.g. he longed to be part of/play for the team
      NB Candidate must make reference to being in the team
    - "He yearned ... to progress" e.g. he longed to improve
    - "He yearned to... read out... (one of the honours of making the team)" e.g. he longed for his moment of glory

    *NB Candidate must refer to the intensity of the desire at least once if dealing with any of the **final three bullet points** (above).*

3. Any six points.

    Glosses of:

    - "98 per cent fail to make the transition (into professional football)"/"only a fraction made it (into professional football)" e.g. very few succeed
    - "Of those who made it into the district team, only a handful were picked by Reading, the local club"/"Perhaps none made it all the way to the

top flight" e.g. even those who have some success didn't make it all the way/some progress doesn't necessarily mean success

- "Many struggle to cope with rejection" e.g. many find it hard to come to terms with not being accepted
- "many suffer anxiety" e.g. they are affected by stress
- "many suffer ...a loss of confidence" e.g. self-esteem/self-belief is undermined
- "and, in some cases, depression" e.g. more serious mental health issues may develop
- "These youngsters are often described as being "left on football's scrapheap"" e.g. (inference) the process is heartless/rigorous/unfeeling
- "it seems to me, though, that the number rejected is, in fact, far higher" e.g. those not selected exceeds number reported
- "the sifting process starts from the first time you kick a ball at the local park" e.g. selection begins very early/there are many stages of filtering/selection
- "the standard was high" e.g. the ability requirement is considerable
- "I remember my heart beating out of my chest when the 'scouts' arrived" e.g. situation causes nerves/pressure
- "I was crushed by the disappointment" e.g. the distress (at failure) is overwhelming
- "the race" e.g. the process is highly competitive
- "... had only just started" e.g. the process is lengthy

4. • "Just as ... so" structure may, but need not, be employed (1+1) e.g. just as there are many grains of sand on the beach so there are many people who don't succeed/are trying to succeed

OR

- Any two areas of similarity. Ideas in common include multiplicity/identical or similar quality/anonymity/ insignificance/expendability/idea of being influenced by another/external/powerful force

5. 1 mark for any one reference; 1 mark for comment (×2).

Possible answers include:

Word choice:

- "inevitable" makes clear the unavoidability of failure
- "natural selection" or "evolution" makes clear e.g. survival of the fittest/that this is a process that has always existed
- "part and parcel" – makes clear the essential nature/necessity of the process of selection

Imagery:

- "first lap"/"final straight"/reference to image of "race" – makes clear notion of a race/different stages of the process

  NB Do not reward a comment on "race" if the same word has been used as a reference.

Sentence structure:

- "But this is football."/"This is life."/short sentence(s) makes clear e.g. the fundamental/ inarguable truth

- repetition of "this is" makes clear e.g. that this is a statement of fact/inescapable
- repetition of "failure is..." makes clear e.g. the fact that success is not universal
- "Without losers, there cannot be winners."/"Without pain, there cannot be joy."/"Without natural selection, there cannot be evolution."/reference to balance/contrast of opposites makes clear e.g. that life has ups and downs
- "Without losers, there cannot be winners. Without pain, there cannot be joy. Without natural selection, there cannot be evolution."/similarity/antithetical construction (within or in consecutive sentence(s))/ parallel structure makes clear e.g. that life has ups and downs
- "Failure is not the opposite of progress; failure is part and parcel of progress."/use of semi-colon makes clear e.g. failure is crucial to moving on

  NB If no reference given, any comment cannot be rewarded.

  NB For full marks two different language features must be dealt with.

6. Any three points.

Possible answers include:

- "The skills are transparent" the criteria for success are obvious
- "the opportunities exist" gives idea of chances being widely available
- "There is no room for family favours" gives idea of lack of nepotism
- "or cosy alliances" gives idea of lack of favourable treatment
- "The best of the best shine through" gives idea of the most talented individuals do make it
- "whether they are from a tough part of Liverpool, like Wayne Rooney, or raised in grinding poverty in Uruguay, like Luis Suárez" gives idea of irrelevance of background

7. Any five points.

Glosses of:

- "Youngsters who are educated and self-assured are likely to be better footballers, too" e.g. young people who have done well at school AND who are confident will perform more effectively
- "The Ancient Greeks understood this only too well" e.g. it has been known for a long time
- "(the humane idea) that the mind and body grow together" e.g. that emotional and physical development go hand in hand
- "The German football system has embraced this truth, too" e.g. this is recognised abroad
- "Such a cultural transformation needs to happen here, too" e.g. the lessons learned abroad should be considered in Britain
- "It is that we need to redefine our relationship with failure" e.g. we must reappraise how we view failure
- "not just in football but in life" e.g. we need to rethink how we deal with failure in areas other than football

- "losing is an essential (indeed, a beautiful) part of life" e.g. experiencing failure is necessary/natural
- "beautiful" e.g. failure can be viewed positively
- "the empowering idea that failure is less important, infinitely less so, than how we respond to it" e.g. how we react to failure is crucial/gives us strength/inspiration
- "Failing (to make the grade at football) is crushing" e.g. not being accepted (as a footballer) is devastating
- "It is natural to be sad" e.g. misery is to be expected/part of what we are
- "But it is also a pathway to a new reality" e.g. but leads us to a different life

    NB Candidates may use the word 'failure' in their response without penalty.

8. 1 mark for any one reference; 1 mark for comment.

    Possible answers include:

    - Similarity of sentence openings/rule of three construction/"Tens of thousands … Hundreds of thousands … Tens of millions" highlights idea of scale/size of competition
    - "But" highlights the shift towards the positive side to failure
    - Short sentence/"But this is not the end of life."/"It is merely the beginning." highlights that all is not lost
    - Repetition of "a new"/rule of three construction/climactic structure/"a new dream, a new hope, a new way of finding meaning" highlights the possibility of a fresh start

    NB Do not accept list.

9. 1 mark for any one selection from lines 60–64; 1 mark for linked reference or explanation from elsewhere.

    Possible answers include:

    - reference to Mark/relates to earlier mentions of Mark
    - use of first person/relates to earlier use of first person
    - "failures (in football)" revisits important idea expressed by e.g. "never made it onto the school team" etc
    - "so important, so trivial"/"Life is too short, too precious, to be derailed by failure" revisits important idea expressed by e.g. "failing to make the grade at football is crushing … but it is also the pathway to a new reality"

    NB Answer may address the idea of importance or triviality.

    - "never deterred him" revisits important idea expressed by e.g. "He kept trying"
    - "new dreams"/"new aspirations" repeats earlier use of word/idea
    - "accept" repeats earlier use of word/idea
    - "embrace" repeats earlier use of word/idea
    - reference to a linguistic element from the final paragraph, e.g. repetition of word "too"/"we have"/sentence structure/short sentences/short paragraph(s) suggests emphatic nature of final summing up comments

    NB do not reward a response that simply says 'it sums up the main ideas of the passage, etc.' unless the candidate goes on to explain what the main idea is.

CRITICAL READING

SECTION 1 — SCOTTISH TEXT

PART A — DRAMA — *Bold Girls* by Rona Munro

1. Any four points for 1 mark each.

    Candidates should use their own words.

    Possible answers include:

    - the women's lives can be disrupted by authoritative raids
    - they accept raids as part of life
    - the women's lives are mundane and a 'simple' night out can be looked forward to
    - the women speak frankly to each other
    - the women know their life style is not healthy
    - the omen are supportive of each other
    - Marie, Cassie and Nora are suspicious of Deirdre
    - there is tension between Cassie and Deirdre
    - Nora uses domesticity to comfort herself from the harshness of reality

2. 1 mark for reference; 1 mark for comment.

    Possible examples of humour include:

    - "It's the D.Ts" suggests irreverence/laughing at herself
    - "… the film stars have"/"Me and Joan Collins both" suggests exaggeration/mock self-importance
    - "… all the excitement" suggests sarcasm
    - "… would your manicure stand up to the closest inspection" suggests irony

3. (a) 1 mark for reference; 1 mark for comment.

    Possible answers include:

    - "Let's see Marie's hand there." suggests good humour between them
    - "Ah she's got a clear conscience." indicates respect for Marie
    - "Wired up but not plugged in." suggests humour/banter

    (b) 1 mark for reference; 1 mark for comment.

    Possible answers include:

    - "black wee heart"/"thieve the clothes"/"nail the wee snake down"/"… if it is Deirdre?" shows Cassie distrusts Deirdre
    - "It is." shows Deirdre stands up to Cassie
    - "I hope you've not taken a fancy… your eye" shows lack of trust

4. 1 mark for reference; 1 mark for comment.

    Possible answers include:

    - "What?" shows confrontation/confusion/defensiveness
    - "That I saw you before." shows accusation/confrontation
    - "you're a lying hoor…" shows the anger/hostility Cassie feels towards Deirdre
    - "…you never saw anything." shows defiance/threat/denial
    - Any part of "With a man. With him. With — " suggests build up to revelation

- Identification of ellipsis suggests anticipation
- Any reference to "Cassie lunges at her before she can get another word out" suggests desperation to stop her/aggression

5. Candidates are likely to include many different aspects of the mother–daughter theme.

   Possible areas for comment include:

   - Despite Nora and Cassie's 'bickering' they constantly support each other (especially with domestic hardships/challenges)
   - Hostilities due to memories of past relationship with father
   - Marie and Deirdre are likely to form a 'mother/daughter' relationship despite the fact they are not directly blood relatives
   - Nora and Cassie 'mother' Marie as they see her as a lone parent left in difficult circumstances (i.e. widowed and alone)
   - Deirdre and her biological mother are not close (as demonstrated by the fact that Deirdre is the victim of domestic violence perpetrated by her mother's latest boyfriend)

   Candidates may choose to answer in **bullet points** in this final question, or write a number of linked statements. There is **no requirement** to write a "mini essay".

   Up to 2 marks can be achieved for identifying elements of commonality as requested in the question. A further 2 marks can be achieved for **reference to the extract given**.

   4 additional marks can be awarded for similar references to **at least one other part of the text**.

   In practice this means:

   Identification of commonality (e.g.: theme, central relationship, importance of setting, use of imagery, development in characterisation, use of personal experience, use of narrative style or any other key element…)

   From the extract:

   1 relevant reference to technique; 1 appropriate comment

   OR 1 relevant reference to idea; 1 appropriate comment

   OR 1 relevant reference to feature; 1 appropriate comment

   OR 1 relevant reference to text; 1 appropriate comment

   (maximum of 2 marks only for discussion of extract)

   from at **least one other part of the text:**

   as above (×2) for **up to 4 marks**.

PART A — DRAMA — *Sailmaker* by Alan Spence

6. 1 mark for identifying an aspect of Alec's attitude; 1 mark for supporting reference (×2).

   Possible answers include:

   - Alec is trying to understand his father e.g. by asking about his dad's reasons for gambling
   - Alec has some admiration for his dad in the past e.g. memories of him making things/working as a Sailmaker
   - Alec tries to encourage Davie e.g. to return to Sailmaking/to move elsewhere/to use his skills to create other products to sell

- Alec has accepted his dad for who he is/his likely relationship with his dad e.g. doesn't argue with Davie's (often unsatisfactory) responses/allows him to throw things of importance onto the fire

7. 1 mark for reference; 1 mark for comment (×2).

   Possible answers include:

   - "(Ah worked on the) Queen Mary (ye know)" e.g. suggests pride/sense of importance
   - "Worked on destroyers durin the war" suggests vivid memories (of usefulness)
   - Reference to list/"Made gun-covers, awnings, tarpaulins" suggests excitement at remembering detail/extent of work
   - "Made a shopping bag for yer mother"/"Made you a swing!"(1) suggests pleasure at creating gifts/versatility of trade
   - "Wi a big sorta…" suggests detailed memory

8. 1 mark for reference; 1 mark for comment (×2).

   Possible answers include:

   - "Nae demand" suggests skills are not needed
   - "Was different durin the War" suggests times have changed
   - "(Been goin) downhill" circumstances have worsened
   - "Yards shuttin doon" suggests no market/employment opportunities for his trade
   - "big empty space" place of work has literally gone
   - "covered wi weeds" suggests neglect
   - "redundancy money" suggests workers have been laid off/unemployment
   - "the manmade fibres"/"usin machines"/"Got lassies daein hauf the work" suggests original trade has changed beyond recognition
   - "Dead loss" suggests no hope for old trade

9. *Possible areas for comment include:*

   From the extract:

   - Negative/pessimistic/lacking motivation
   - Seen to be different before the death of his wife e.g. making bags and toys, working hard as an apprentice.
   - Stage directions e.g. (shrugs)
   - Negative language ("backed a loser right fae the start" and "Dead loss" etc)

   From elsewhere:

   - Answers will likely focus on Davie's downwards spiral from that start of the play triggered by his inability to cope with the death of his wife, which led to gambling and drinking.
   - He also struggled to cope with being a single parent to Alec, and their home situation was often unsatisfactory (e.g. provision for meals and clothing as well as the generally untidy nature of the home).
   - His employment situation changed from Sailmaker (before the play) to "tick man" to sweeper to eventually unemployed, all reflecting his decline in status/self-esteem.
   - He is seen as someone who always procrastinates (e.g. doing up the yacht, tidying the house) and who cannot move on (e.g. inability to be truthful about romantic interests).

- He is seen to be intelligent (e.g. discussing literature or religion) but he never uses this or his Sailmaking skills to try and improve his situation.

- He lacks the ability to be pro-active about his situation and feels that he is always unlucky.

- Despite these failings, he constantly encourages Alec to look for something better in life and encourages him to find this through education and employment.

Candidates may choose to answer in **bullet points** in this final question, or write a number of linked statements. There is **no requirement** to write a "mini essay".

Up to 2 marks can be achieved for identifying elements of commonality as requested in the question. A further 2 marks can be achieved for **reference to the extract given.**

4 additional marks can be awarded for similar references to **at least one other part of the text.**

In practice this means:

Identification of commonality (e.g.: theme, central relationship, importance of setting, use of imagery, development in characterisation, use of personal experience, use of narrative style or any other key element…)

From the extract:

1 relevant reference to technique; 1 appropriate comment

OR 1 relevant reference to idea; 1 appropriate comment

OR 1 relevant reference to feature; 1 appropriate comment

OR 1 relevant reference to text; 1 appropriate comment

(**maximum of 2 marks only for discussion of extract)**

from at **least one other part of the text:**

as above (×2) for **up to 4 marks.**

PART A — DRAMA — *Tally's Blood* by Ann Marie Di Mambro

10. Candidates should make four key points for 1 mark each.

Candidates may choose to make four separate summary points or may give both sides of two areas of disagreement.

Possible answers include:

- Rosinella thinks Hughie and Lucia are in love/developing romantic feelings; but Massimo thinks they are just friends

- Massimo thinks Lucia is upset about not getting to the wedding; but Rosinella thinks it's more than that

- Massimo thinks there is no harm in her asking to go to the wedding; but Rosinella thinks it is concerning

- Massimo thinks that Rosinella is too overbearing/interfering/worrying too much; but Rosinella thinks she hasn't done enough to prevent this

- Rosinella is determined to prevent their relationship developing further; but Massimo does not want to get involved in it

11. 1 mark for reference; 1 mark for comment (×2).

Possible answers include:

- "She's to marry an Italian" suggests Rosinella's single mindedness/insistence

- "I don't worry enough" suggests over protectiveness

- "It's been going on before my eyes" suggests paranoia/suspicion

- "It's bad enough he's fell for her" suggests her dislike of Hughie

- "I'll soon put a stop to this before it starts" suggests her determination

- "Italians are not interested …" suggests her prejudiced views

- short sentences suggest her blunt/frank/straight to the point nature

12. 1 mark for identifying an attitude for each character; 1 mark for supporting reference (×2).

Possible answers include:

Rosinella:

- "Are you forgetting what this country did…?" suggests anger/bitterness/inability to let go

- "They took you" suggests sense of injustice

- "as if you were a thief" suggests she feels Massimo's treatment was terrible/unforgivable

- "I'll never get over it" suggests she feels that the trauma was too much to bear/she will hold a grudge forever

Massimo:

- "all I care about the war is that it's over" suggests he wants to move on from it/forget about it

- "I lost ma faither, ma brother" suggests that he has a deep sadness/genuine grief at loss of family

- "I lost … four years out ma life" suggests great sadness/resentment at losing his liberty

- "everybody suffered"/"Not just us" suggests he accepts that grudges are pointless/the trauma is shared

13. *Possible areas for comment include:*

From the extract:

- Massimo is quiet, forgiving, unaware, private, patient, in love with Rosinella, etc.

From elsewhere:

- Shows kindness e.g. by giving Hughie a job, offering him an ice cream van, giving Bridget money, etc.

- Shows patience e.g. with Rosinella's constant comments, interfering, bossing about, etc.

- Shows he is hard working e.g. works long hours in the shop while Rosinella and Lucia go out and spend, etc.

- Shows love towards Rosinella e.g. romantic story of their elopement (which he re-enacts at the end of the play), affectionately calls her "Rosie", etc.

- Suffers e.g. shop is attacked/has racist remarks made towards him, is taken hostage during the war, doesn't have a child of his own, etc.

Candidates may choose to answer in **bullet points** in this final question, or write a number of linked statements. There is **no requirement** to write a "mini essay".

Up to 2 marks can be achieved for identifying elements of commonality as requested in the question. A further 2 marks can be achieved for **reference to the extract given.**

4 additional marks can be awarded for similar references to at **least one other part of the text.**

<u>In practice this means:</u>

Identification of commonality (e.g.: theme, central relationship, importance of setting, use of imagery, development in characterisation, use of personal experience, use of narrative style or any other key element...)

From the extract:

1 relevant reference to technique; 1 appropriate comment

OR 1 relevant reference to idea; 1 appropriate comment

OR 1 relevant reference to feature; 1 appropriate comment

OR 1 relevant reference to text; 1 appropriate comment

(maximum of 2 marks only for discussion of extract)

from at **least one other part of the text:**

as above (×2) for **up to 4 marks.**

PART B — PROSE — *The Cone-Gatherers* by Robin Jenkins

14. Any four points for 1 mark each.

Candidates should use their own words as far as possible.

Possible answers include:

- no electric lighting
- there is not much natural light — reference to a single window
- there is little furniture — a box for a table/only two beds
- there are no soft furnishings — newspaper is used instead of a tablecloth
- they make the best of what they have
- the cones being burned — this creates a pleasant smell in the hut
- they have a simple routine e.g. they prepare the vegetables the evening before
- they prepare and eat their meal without washing/ don't change their clothes
- there is little conversation/they are content with the silence/they are exhausted
- they pass the time doing simple things e.g. they have an unvarying routine

15. 1 mark for reference; 1 mark for comment (×2).

Possible answers include:

- "against his will" suggests that Duror is forced to recognise something positive about the cone-gatherers/they are at one with nature
- "final defeat" — word choice suggests that Duror is somehow seeking victory over the cone-gatherers/ thinks he is superior
- "Outwardly ... inwardly" — (balanced) sentence structure OR balance OR contrast suggests the disparity between Duror's external feelings of criticism of Nazi brutality and his inner approval
- "approved" suggests in reality he hates the cone-gatherers/agrees with Hitler's attitudes
- "sensed the kinship between the carver and the creature" suggests jealousy/resentment
- "idiocy" strong word-choice used to illustrate his feelings that Calum is inferior/useless ...

- "idiots"/"imbecile" word-choice cruelly sums up Duror's criticism of Calum mentally
- "cripples"/"freak" word-choice cruelly sums up Duror's criticism of Calum physically

16. 1 mark for reference; 1 mark for comment (×2).

Possible answers include:

- "roused himself and moved away" suggests desire to distance himself
- "something unresolved" suggests lack of closure
- "never cease" suggests endless agony
- "torment" suggests Duror is suffering mentally as this conveys extreme pain/torture
- "he himself was the third" suggests sense of connection
- "he halted and looked back" suggests indecision/ hesitation
- "fists tightened on the gun" suggests that Duror wishes to kill the cone-gatherers/the strength of his hatred
- "kicking" suggests feelings of violence/anger
- "disgust" suggests feelings of hatred/revulsion
- "blasting" suggests he wants to destroy them
- "icy (hand)" suggests his chilling cruelty/feelings of being controlled by fate
- reference to list suggests extreme feelings of violence/aggressive intent
- "hideous" suggests that he knows that his thoughts are wrong
- "liberating" suggests desire to be rid of them
- "fratricide" suggests murderous thoughts

17. *Possible areas for comment include:*

From the extract:

- The scene inside the cone-gatherers' hut is one of peace and tranquillity, with Neil reading the paper and Calum carving a squirrel from wood
- However, the fact that Duror is spying on the brothers and considering killing them is an example of his evil

OR

- The setting inside the hut is homely and pleasant — lamp burning/pleasant smell of burning cones; however, Duror's sympathy with the murders of "idiots and cripples" in the gas-chambers is an example of his evil thoughts

From elsewhere:

Good

- Initial description of idyllic setting makes it seem like a place of tranquillity/a Garden of Eden
- Calum's goodness is referred to throughout the novel — e.g. when Neil tells him he is better than the rest of them
- Roderick's wish to befriend the cone-gatherers/ offer them a lift in the car/defend them to his mother suggests that he, too, is linked with fairness and goodness — he tells his mother "You told me yourself ... never to be quiet if I saw injustice being done."

- Roderick's intention to take the cake to the cone-gatherers as a peace-offering after the beach-hut incident shows his willingness to take responsibility for his mother's wrong
- At the end, Calum is sacrificed for the greater good — Lady Runcie-Campbell's tears represent her understanding of this

Evil

- Duror's presence in the wood is representative of the snake in the Garden of Eden — his first appearance shows him with his gun trained on Calum
- Duror's evil lies about Calum represent his wish to damage Calum's reputation and have him thrown out of the wood
- Duror's mental illness is described in metaphors of diseased/dying trees to show how such evil can destroy a strong person
- Duror's murder of Calum and his own suicide at the end illustrate the consequences of his evil

Candidates may choose to answer in **bullet points** in this final question, or write a number of linked statements. There is **no requirement** to write a "mini essay".

Up to 2 marks can be achieved for identifying elements of commonality as requested in the question. A further 2 marks can be achieved for **reference to the extract given.**

4 additional marks can be awarded for similar references to at **least one other part of the text.**

In practice this means:

Identification of commonality (e.g.: theme, central relationship, importance of setting, use of imagery, development in characterisation, use of personal experience, use of narrative style or any other key element…)

From the extract:

1 relevant reference to technique; 1 appropriate comment

OR 1 relevant reference to idea; 1 appropriate comment

OR 1 relevant reference to feature; 1 appropriate comment

OR 1 relevant reference to text; 1 appropriate comment

(maximum of 2 marks only for discussion of extract)

from at **least one other part of the text:**

as above (×2) for **up to 4 marks.**

PART B — PROSE — *The Testament of Gideon Mack* by James Robertson

18. Any three points for 1 mark each.

Possible answers include:

- the Devil speaks in a down to earth way
- the Devil seems vulnerable
- the Devil seems courteous/polite
- the Devil can be funny
- the Devil is the opposite to what you expect
- the Devil has some form of affection for Scotland
- the Devil is fond of telling stories about his travels/adventures/impressions of people and places
- the Devil enjoys the depressive nature of the people in Scotland
- the Devil likes the terrible weather (in Scotland)

- the Devil is an astute commentator on changes in society
- the Devil subverts biblical texts/ideas
- the Devil can be changeable

19. 1 mark for reference; 1 mark for comment.

Possible answers include:

- "I made no further protest"/"I couldn't help it" suggests contrition
- "terrible arm" suggests terror
- "I shrank away" suggests avoidance
- "terrified" suggests intense fear
- "clutching" suggests tension
- "I closed my eyes" suggests trepidation

20. Any three points for 1 mark each.

Possible answers include:

- Devil puts his hand in the fire; until it is very hot; then he comes towards Mack's leg with the hot arm
- Mack feels a strange sensation in his leg
- the Devil's hand is placed under Mack's skin
- the skin looks like it is burning/feels like it is on fire
- the Devil manipulates the bone; back in alignment; and sticks it back together
- the process is painless

21. Candidates must address two different aspects.

1 mark for reference; 1 mark for comment (×2).

Possible answers include:

- annoyed/grumpy or similar shown by "sparked up a bit"/"snapped"
- assertive/taking control or similar shown by repetition of "don't think"
- nostalgic/warm or similar shown by stories of North Berwick and/or Auchtermuchty/(repetition of) "I like Scotland"/any example of why he likes Scotland
- sad/down in the dumps or similar shown by "morose"/"fed up"
- cheerful/happy or similar shown by "brightened"
- vulnerable/needy or similar shown by "please"/"I'd like to"
- focused/intent or similar shown by "(intense) concentration"/"fully three minutes"/general comment on his focus when fixing the leg

22. Candidates should identify one aspect of Mack's character in this extract and go on to discuss how this is developed elsewhere in the novel. It should be at least implied that the character traits are as a result of meeting the Devil.

Accept also events which follow the meeting in the cave which are a direct result of the meeting eg Catherine's funeral, his seeming madness, his being 'struck off', his disappearance but links must be made in the explanation to the meeting with the Devil.

Possible aspects of character include:

- arrogance — e.g. he has suffered a near death experience as well as meeting the devil, and survived, which makes him feel untouchable, all powerful or similar as exemplified elsewhere in the novel in his dealings with the community, interested parties, etc. (before the meeting with the Devil, Mack is portrayed as a weak and cowardly character);

- self-righteousness — e.g. he has seen things that others have not and he wants to tell everyone about this as exemplified at Catherine's funeral; argumentative/contrariness — e.g. refusal to back down in the face of huge opposition later in the book, resulting in him being excommunicated;

- air of mystery — e.g. he keeps himself to himself and/or eventually disappears completely.

Candidates may choose to answer in **bullet points** in this final question, or write a number of linked statements. There is **no requirement** to write a "mini essay".

Up to 2 marks can be achieved for identifying elements of commonality as requested in the question. A further 2 marks can be achieved for **reference to the extract given**.

4 additional marks can be awarded for similar references to at **least one other part of the text**.

<u>In practice this means:</u>

Identification of commonality (e.g.: theme, central relationship, importance of setting, use of imagery, development in characterisation, use of personal experience, use of narrative style or any other key element…)

From the extract:

1 relevant reference to technique; 1 appropriate comment

OR 1 relevant reference to idea; 1 appropriate comment

OR 1 relevant reference to feature; 1 appropriate comment

OR 1 relevant reference to text; 1 appropriate comment

(maximum of 2 marks only for discussion of extract)

from at **least one other part of the text:**

as above (×2) for **up to 4 marks.**

PART B — PROSE — *Kidnapped* by Robert Louis Stevenson

23. Any four points for 1 mark each.

Possible answers include:

- The sun rises and Alan and David see where they are
- Alan is worried that they will be found at this location
- Alan leaps over the river
- David follows Alan
- They have a large jump to make from the middle rock to the other bank of the river
- David is scared
- Alan is angry at him
- Alan gives David alcohol to calm him
- David initially does not make it
- Alan takes hold of him and pulls him ashore

24. (a) 1 mark for reference; 1 mark for comment.

Possible answers include:

- "ran harder than ever" suggests no one can catch him
- "Alan looked neither to the right or the left" suggests he's oblivious to danger

- "jumped clean upon the middle rock" suggests athletic prowess
- "that rock was small" suggests difficulty doesn't faze him

(b) 1 mark for reference; 1 mark for comment.

Possible answers include:

- "this horrible place" suggests David's unhappiness with the setting
- "horrid thundering" suggests David's anxiety
- "made my belly quake" suggests fear
- "scarce time" suggests panic
- "to understand the peril" suggests necessity of acting quickly

25. 1 mark for sentence structure feature/reference; 1 mark for relevant comment on feature/reference; 1 mark for word choice example; 1 mark for relevant comment on word choice

Possible answers include:

Sentence structure

- Repetition of "I"/repetition of first person pronoun and/or associated verb emphasises dramatic action/ gives a sense of immediacy
- Repetition of "slipped" emphasises the danger and drama as David tries to jump the river
- long sentence (lines 25—28) emphasises the drama of the action through explanation of David's thought process as he faces danger
- long sentence (lines 25—28)/list emphasis of drama through list of actions in long sentence/number of dangers
- listing [any examples from lines 25—28 in particular]; "these slipped, caught again, slipped again"

OR

- "[Alan seized me,] first by the hair, then by the collar" provides a powerful dramatic effect in their speed and immediacy

Word choice

- "alone" emphasises that David may feel isolated and fearful at this point, hence dramatic
- "flung" has connotations of throwing himself with some force, possibly desperate
- "anger" emphasises his strong emotional state
- "despair" connotations of hopelessness which creates dramatic mood
- "seized" emphasises the desperate dramatic action taken by Alan
- "great strain" emphasises the effort required to save David and enhances the drama of the moment
- "dragged" emphasises the weight and dramatic struggle Alan had to bring David to the bank of the river

26. *Possible areas for comment include:*

- Alan's prowess in the roundhouse conflict on the Covenant;
- Alan's gift of the silver button to David;
- Alan's showing David the political realities of the Scottish Highlands;

- Alan assisting David in his journey back to Edinburgh;
- Alan getting the Balquidder safe house;
- Alan convincing girl to row them over the River Forth;
- Alan's contribution in trapping Ebenezer at the end of the novel;
- Alan's friendship enhances David's self-confidence;
- Alan's role in David's life helps in David maturing into a man.

Candidates may choose to answer in **bullet points** in this final question, or write a number of linked statements. There is **no requirement** to write a "mini essay".

Up to 2 marks can be achieved for identifying elements of commonality as requested in the question. A further 2 marks can be achieved for **reference to the extract given**.

4 additional marks can be awarded for similar references to at **least one other part of the text**.

In practice this means:

Identification of commonality (e.g.: theme, central relationship, importance of setting, use of imagery, development in characterisation, use of personal experience, use of narrative style or any other key element...)

From the extract:

1 relevant reference to technique; 1 appropriate comment

OR 1 relevant reference to idea; 1 appropriate comment

OR 1 relevant reference to feature; 1 appropriate comment

OR 1 relevant reference to text; 1 appropriate comment

(**maximum of 2 marks only for discussion of extract**)

from at **least one other part of the text**:

as above (×2) for **up to 4 marks**.

PART B — PROSE — *The Crater* by Iain Crichton Smith

27. 1 mark for reference; 1 mark for comment (×2).

Possible answers include:

- "squirmed" suggests unease/discomfort/difficulty in moving
- (blunt statement) "I am frightened" highlights the danger he faced
- repetition (of "fear") conveys the overpowering nature of his feelings
- "grey figures" suggests his terror of the unknown/unfamiliar
- "darkness" conveys his helplessness/despair about his situation
- enemy "crawling beneath" suggests his deep-rooted/inner emotions
- spider's web suggests his horror of being caught/trapped/killed by the enemy

28. Any four points for 1 mark each.

Possible answers include:

- the commotion/confusion ("thrustings and flashes")
- the difficulty in determining reality from illusion ("saw or imagined he saw")
- the threat from explosives and weapons ("Mills bombs/bayonets")

- the vermin ("scurryings...rats")
- the individual danger of face-to-face combat ("face towered above him")
- the disgusting conditions ("terrible stink")
- the brutality/violence ("flowing of blood")
- the likelihood of being killed

29. Candidates should identify an example of sentence structure and comment on how this conveys the danger faced by the men.

1 mark for reference; 1 mark for comment.

Possible answers include:

- single word sentence "Back" suggests the pressure of the moment
- repetition of "back" conveys the frantic atmosphere/unsafe/unstable environment
- minor sentence "Over the parapet" shows the threat/risk/exposed/fragile nature of their position
- inversion of "crouched" highlights their vulnerability/helplessness (in the face of enemy fire)
- repetition of "and" **OR** list of actions "crouched/run/scrambled" suggests the many difficulties in reaching safety

30. 1 mark for reference; 1 mark for comment.

Possible answers include:

- "there is no point" the men's realisation of their gloomy predicament
- "could not tell the expression" suggests their loss of connection/numbness about their situation
- "shells still falling" suggests the ceaseless fighting
- "dead moons" suggests the lack of hope/dark world they inhabit

31. *Possible areas for comment include:*

- "Mother and Son" — the impact of the mother's words e.g. "her bitter barbs passed over him...Most often however they stung him and stood quivering in his flesh" to convey the destructive nature of their relationship
- "The Telegram" — The symbolism of birds e.g. "domestic bird...aquiline ...buzzard" to show the contrasting nature of the two women/convey the theme of sacrifice/constraints of small community/isolation/effects of war
- "The Red Door" — The many references to colour/symbolism of the door/description of the landscape e.g. "the earth was painted with an unearthly glow and the sea was like a strange volume" to highlight Murdo's growing realisation that he does not have to conform
- "In Church" — The religious symbolism and language e.g. "gods were carelessly punching" to convey the devastating effects/futility of war

Candidates may choose to answer in **bullet points** in this final question, or write a number of linked statements. There is **no requirement** to write a "mini essay".

Up to 2 marks can be achieved for identifying elements of commonality as requested in the question. A further 2 marks can be achieved for **reference to the extract given**.

4 additional marks can be awarded for similar references to at **least one other part of the text.**

<u>In practice this means:</u>

Identification of commonality (e.g.: theme, central relationship, importance of setting, use of imagery, development in characterisation, use of personal experience, use of narrative style or any other key element...)

From the extract:

1 relevant reference to technique; 1 appropriate comment

OR 1 relevant reference to idea; 1 appropriate comment

OR 1 relevant reference to feature; 1 appropriate comment

OR 1 relevant reference to text; 1 appropriate comment

(maximum of 2 marks only for discussion of extract)

from at **least one other part of the text:**

as above (×2) for **up to 4 marks.**

PART B — PROSE — *Zimmerobics* by Anne Donovan

32. Two points for 1 mark each.

    Possible answers include:

    - Resigned/uneasy/reluctant/sceptical at the start
    - Cautiously optimistic
    - increasingly confident
    - Completely involved/very pleased with herself/happy/convinced of its benefits

33. 1 mark for reference; 1 mark for comment.

    Possible answers include:

    - "Creaking sounds"/"creaky old joints" suggests lack of agility
    - "shuffled in most cases" suggests caution/slowness
    - "(old and) decrepit" suggests decay/decline
    - "hirpled" suggests difficulty of movement

34. 1 mark for reference; 1 mark for comment (×2).

    Possible answers include:

    - "pleasant tingling in my limbs" suggests enjoyment
    - "I became quite proficient" suggests pride in developing skill
    - "It was brilliant" suggests enthusiasm
    - "(my body) still worked" suggests relief/wonderment
    - "the memory of the exercise class lingered" suggests long lasting impact
    - "I felt better/as though someone had oiled all the creaky old joints" suggests physical benefits
    - "a pleasant ache/an ache of life" suggests love of life

35. 1 mark for reference; 1 mark for comment (×2).

    Possible answers include:

    - Reference to school uniform suggests comic embarrassment
    - "Cheryl bounced" suggests over-energetic movement, or similar comment on humorous connotations of word choice
    - ("wearing a pair of trainers that made her) feet look like horse's hooves" suggests clumsiness/ungainliness, or similar comment on the incongruity of the image applied to a fitness instructor

- Detailed description of the outfit over the top attention to detail
- "I hope she doesn't need to go to the toilet in a hurry" humorous comment on impractical nature of outfit
- Lengthy/detailed/exaggerated description of routine/understanding of implication of high level of skill in contrast with the limited activity actually done
- Parenthetical comment/"(well, shuffled in most cases)" plus comment on mocking tone/self-deprecating humour
- Hyperbole/"boldly" to describe a simple action
- juxtaposition of "boldly" and "zimmer-frames" incongruous nature of the two terms
- Word choice/"shuffled"/"hirpled" in contrast with words you would expect to describe exercise movements, implying energy, grace or skill

36. *Possible areas for comment include:*

- "All that Glisters" — any aspect or development of Clare's relationship with her father such as her desire to make her father happy with the card she makes at school; Clare's concern for her father's deteriorating health; the closeness between Clare and her father shown through her explanation of "subtle", and the way she defies her aunt at the end of the story, to do what her father would have liked; Clare's creativity shown through how she applies the pens to card early in the story and to herself at the end; Clare's determination to obtain the pens and the sacrifice she is prepared to make to afford them; Clare's shocked reaction to her father's death; the conflict between Clare and the shop assistant and her aunt. Use of first person narrative/dialect/informal register/simple word choice to bring authenticity/help the reader understand Clare's thoughts and feelings.

- "Virtual Pals" — use of emails/first person narrative allows the reader to understand Siobhan's thoughts/to see her becoming more confident. Use of simple sentence structure, word choice and dialect reflect her age/experience/interests, etc. Themes such as friendship and trust, and boyfriend issues are typical teenage concerns, creating authenticity.

- "Dear Santa" — use of first person narrative/dialect/informal register/simple word choice to reveal Alison's feelings (e.g. unloved by her mother, overlooked by her father, jealous of her sister and worthless overall), and to show Alison is growing up and changing in the references to Santa. Use of imagery to reveal her feelings for her mother, her sister, and about herself. Use of example/anecdote to show her feelings about Katie/herself.

- "A Chitterin Bite" — use of contrasting registers to highlight differences in character between young and adult Mary. Use of informal register to reflect Mary's character as a child. Use of standard English to show adult Mary has changed. Use of two time frames to allow the reader to see the change in how Mary reacts to being let down as a child and how she reacts as an adult. Use of symbolism of the "chitterin bite" to show Mary's character changing — initially, comforting, associated with friendship, then chokes her, associated with rejection, then a symbol for her revenge and ability to move on.

- "Away in a Manger" — use of dialect to make Sandra's and Amy's characters convincing; use of dialogue to create convincing parent child relationship; use of dialogue to demonstrate love between Sandra and Amy; Sandra's and Amy's different attitudes to the nativity to show the difference between a child's and an adult's perspective.

Candidates may choose to answer in **bullet points** in this final question, or write a number of linked statements. There is **no requirement** to write a "mini essay".

Up to 2 marks can be achieved for identifying elements of commonality as requested in the question. A further 2 marks can be achieved for **reference to the extract given.**

4 additional marks can be awarded for similar references to at **least one other part of the text.**

<u>In practice this means:</u>

Identification of commonality (e.g.: theme, central relationship, importance of setting, use of imagery, development in characterisation, use of personal experience, use of narrative style or any other key element…)

From the extract:

1 relevant reference to technique; 1 appropriate comment

OR 1 relevant reference to idea; 1 appropriate comment

OR 1 relevant reference to feature; 1 appropriate comment

OR 1 relevant reference to text; 1 appropriate comment

(maximum of 2 marks only for discussion of extract)

from at **least one other part of the text:**

as above (×2) for **up to 4 marks.**

PART C — POETRY — *War Photographer* by Carol Ann Duffy

37. 1 mark for reference; 1 mark for comment.

Possible answers include:

- "darkroom"/"finally alone" suggests confessional
- "suffering" suggests passion/pain/key concern of religion, etc.
- "(set out in) ordered rows" suggests lines of pews/bibles, etc.
- "The only light is red"/"softly glows" suggests ever-present illumination (often from a candle) in some churches
- "preparing to intone" suggests that the photographer's tasks (in developing photographs) reminds the poet of a priest's ritual
- "Mass" suggests religious ceremony
- "All flesh is grass" is a Biblical reference

38. Candidates should include one example from each side (home country & countries visited).

1 mark for reference; 1 mark for comment (×2).

Possible answers include:

Home country:

- "Home again" suggests relief at returning/comfort/security
- "Rural England" suggests peaceful countryside

- Short/minor sentence (of "Rural England.") suggests isolation from harm/conflict, etc.
- "ordinary pain" suggests any discomforts are bearable
- "simple weather" suggests climate is constant/predictable/not dramatic

Countries visited:

- "explode beneath the feet" suggests violence/unexpected, dramatic happenings
- "running" suggests imminent danger
- "running children" even young people are under threat
- "nightmare" suggests terror/fear/sleeplessness
- "nightmare heat" suggests discomfort/reference to napalm attacks/extreme weather

39. 1 mark for reference; 1 mark for comment (×2).

Possible answers include:

- "Something is happening."/dramatic short sentence suggests emergence of strong recollection
- "twist (before his eyes)" suggests painful image
- "half-formed ghost" suggests photographer is haunted by memories
- "cries (of this man's wife)" suggests potent/strong/disturbing sounds
- "blood" suggests disturbing/violent image
- "stained into foreign dust" suggests permanent impression

40. Two points for 1 mark each. Candidates should use their own words.

Possible answers include:

- Only a small selection of the photographs are revealed to the public
- Futility of photographer's effort
- Readers don't pay sufficient attention to the scale of suffering/carry on with lives regardless
- Readers are insufficiently emotionally engaged
- Photographer has become hardened
- The world has become numb to conflict

41. *Possible areas for comment include:*

- "Havisham" — main character suffers due to painful memories of wedding day.
- "Originally" — suffering due to moving to unfamiliar place. Suffering perhaps due to questions of identity. Also idea of moving on from suffering and revising identity.
- "Mrs Midas" — main character suffers due to behaviour/obsessions of her partner.
- "Valentine" — potential pain and suffering caused by love.
- "Anne Hathaway" — loss felt at Shakespeare's absence from her life. She is left just with memories.

Candidates may choose to answer in **bullet points** in this final question, or write a number of linked statements. There is **no requirement** to write a "mini essay".

Up to 2 marks can be achieved for identifying elements of commonality as requested in the question. A further 2 marks can be achieved for **reference to the extract given.**

4 additional marks can be awarded for similar references to at **least one other poem by Duffy.**

In practice this means:

Identification of commonality (e.g.: theme, central relationship, importance of setting, use of imagery, development in characterisation, use of personal experience, use of narrative style or any other key element…)

From the extract:

1 relevant reference to technique; 1 appropriate comment

OR 1 relevant reference to idea; 1 appropriate comment

OR 1 relevant reference to feature; 1 appropriate comment

OR 1 relevant reference to text; 1 appropriate comment

(maximum of 2 marks only for discussion of extract)

from at **least one other poem:**

as above (×2) for **up to 4 marks.**

PART C — POETRY — *Trio* by Edwin Morgan

42. 1 mark for reference; 1 mark for comment.

    Possible answers include:

    - "quickly" suggests vitality/liveliness
    - "Christmas lights" suggests festive/celebration/ happy time of year
    - "new (guitar)" suggests happiness of giving/receiving
    - "(very young) baby" suggests happiness of new birth
    - "(the three of them are) laughing" suggests happiness/enjoyment
    - "(their breath) rises" suggests uplifting moment
    - "(in a cloud of) happiness" suggests delight/enjoyment
    - "'Wait till he sees this but!'" suggests eagerness/ delight

43. 1 mark for reference; 1 mark for comment.

    Possible answers include:

    - "baby" suggests new birth
    - "white (shawl)" suggests purity
    - "bright (eyes)" suggests clarity/purity
    - "fresh (sweet cake)" suggests newness/unspoiled
    - "milky (plastic cover)" suggests whiteness
    - "silver tinsel tape"/"sprig of mistletoe" suggest Christmas time, which is a celebration of new birth

44. 1 mark for reference; 1 mark for comment (×2).

    Possible answers include:

    - "…powerless before you" suggests that nothing can stop them
    - "you put paid" suggests that they conquer
    - "(put paid) to fate" suggests that even a seemingly unstoppable force (fate) cannot stand in the way of them
    - "…it abdicates" suggests the group compels the opposition to give up
    - "Monsters" suggests that the group is prepared to stand up to fearsome opposition
    - "(Monsters of the year) go blank" suggests that opposition freezes/has no solution

- "are scattered back" suggests that the opposition surrenders
- "can't bear" suggests that nothing can stand/endure the force of the group
- "march" suggests that the group has the strength of an army

45. 1 mark for reference; 1 mark for comment (×2).

    Possible answers include:

    - "yet not vanished" suggests the group will not disappear/will keep going/they will be there in spirit but not physically there
    - "for in their arms they wind the life of men and beasts" suggests that the group is important to/stand for all nature/humanity/continuity/persistence
    - "music" suggests celebration, etc.
    - "laughter (ringing them round)" suggests happiness
    - "at the end of this winter's day" suggests that the group represents the end of winter/moving on to Spring, etc.

46. *Possible areas for comment include:*

    - "Hyena" — the setting of African dry lands is important in establishing how the hyena fits in with/ relates to its environment.
    - "In the Snack-bar" — the setting of the Snack-bar is crucial to Morgan's depiction of the difficulties faced by the old man.
    - "Good Friday" — the setting of the bus/Glasgow is central to Morgan's central concerns of class differences, etc. Setting in time of Easter is central to concerns of religion.
    - "Winter" — the setting of Bingham's Pond/West End of Glasgow is important in Morgan's exploration of themes of death and time.
    - "Slate" — Morgan uses the setting of Scotland's mountains/landscape to consider themes of time/ nationhood, etc.

Candidates may choose to answer in **bullet points** in this final question, or write a number of linked statements. There is **no requirement** to write a "mini essay".

Up to 2 marks can be achieved for identifying elements of commonality as requested in the question. A further 2 marks can be achieved for **reference to the extract given.**

4 additional marks can be awarded for similar references to at **least one other poem by Morgan.**

In practice this means:

Identification of commonality (e.g.: theme, central relationship, importance of setting, use of imagery, development in characterisation, use of personal experience, use of narrative style or any other key element…)

From the extract:

1 relevant reference to technique; 1 appropriate comment

OR 1 relevant reference to idea; 1 appropriate comment

OR 1 relevant reference to feature; 1 appropriate comment

OR 1 relevant reference to text; 1 appropriate comment

(maximum of 2 marks only for discussion of extract)

from at **least one other poem:**

as above (×2) for **up to 4 marks.**

PART C — POETRY — *Aunt Julia* by Norman MacCaig

47. 1 mark for reference; 1 mark for comment.

NB: Do not award a mark for "frustration" as this is in the question.

Possible answers include:

- "(Aunt Julia spoke) Gaelic" suggests that there is a language barrier between Aunt Julia and the poet
- "very loud and very fast" repetition emphasises the difficulties of understanding
- "loud" suggests annoyance at high volume
- "fast" speed caused difficulties in understanding
- "I could not...I could not" repetition emphasises the fact that the poet is conscious of his own inadequacies in communicating with Aunt Julia
- "(I could not) answer her" suggests poet's inability to reply/communicate
- "(I could not) understand her" suggests poet's lack of comprehension

48. 1 mark for reference; 1 mark for comment (×2).

NB: Do not reward the same analytical comment given twice for two different references.

Possible answers include:

- "(She wore) men's boots" suggests her unconventional dress/work ethic
- "(when she wore) any" suggests poverty/hardiness
- "strong (foot)" suggests physical capabilities
- "stained with peat" suggests lack of vanity/work ethic/she is at one with the land
- "paddling with...while her right hand" suggests dexterity/high level of skill
- "marvellously (out of the air)" suggests almost magical abilities
- "Hers"/"(Hers) was the only house" suggests uniqueness/sense of security
- "crickets being friendly" suggests peace/contentment
- "(She was) buckets"/"water flouncing into them" suggests plenty/abundance of natural resources/she was almost "elemental"
- "She was winds..." suggests that she represents the island gales
- "(She was) brown eggs" suggests nature/crofting life
- "black skirts" suggests she represented typical island dress of the time
- "(keeper of) threepennybits" suggests habits of economy/savings/combating poverty

49. 1 mark for reference; 1 mark for comment (×2).

Possible answers include:

- "(By the time) I had learned a little" suggests regret at time passing/lateness of learning
- "silenced" is associated with death/contrasts with earlier volume of Aunt Julia
- "absolute black" suggests death/darkness/oblivion/loss
- "sandy grave" suggests death

50. 1 mark for reference from specified lines; 1 mark for reference from elsewhere/comment on ideas or technique. Points/references must match up.

Possible answers include:

- "getting angry, getting angry" echoes repetition employed at various points in the poem/identification of an example of repetition e.g. "very loud and very fast"
- "getting angry" echoes dissatisfaction expressed earlier in the poem/identification of example e.g. "I could not...etc."
- "questions unanswered" echoes earlier communication problems/identification of example e.g. "I could not understand her, etc."
- "But I hear her still" echoes earlier reference to her voice/reference to her ever present nature
- "seagull's voice" echoes earlier reference to "very loud", "loud", "fast" etc.
- "peatscrapes and lazy beds" echoes earlier reference to landscape/"stained with peat"

51. *Possible areas for comment include:*

- "Visiting Hour" — "white cave of forgetfulness," "distance of pain," "neither she nor I can cross," "books that will not be read," etc. are all references to being separated from someone close
- "Assisi" — the beggar is kept separate from/outside of the church and/or the guide's tour of the church
- "Memorial" — separation caused by death. Constant reminders of separation from surroundings, etc.
- "Sounds of the day" — separation made potent by sounds/silences. Long-lasting impact of separation ("quietest fire in the world").
- "Basking Shark" — realisation that humans have separated themselves from nature/origins.

Candidates may choose to answer in **bullet points** in this final question, or write a number of linked statements. There is **no requirement** to write a "mini essay".

Up to 2 marks can be achieved for identifying elements of commonality as requested in the question. A further 2 marks can be achieved for **reference to the extract given**.

4 additional marks can be awarded for similar references to at **least one other poem by MacCaig**.

<u>In practice this means:</u>

Identification of commonality (e.g.: theme, central relationship, importance of setting, use of imagery, development in characterisation, use of personal experience, use of narrative style or any other key element...)

From the extract:

1 relevant reference to technique; 1 appropriate comment

OR 1 relevant reference to idea; 1 appropriate comment

OR 1 relevant reference to feature; 1 appropriate comment

OR 1 relevant reference to text; 1 appropriate comment

(maximum of 2 marks only for discussion of extract)

from at **least one other poem:**

as above (×2) for **up to 4 marks.**

PART C — POETRY — *Bed* by Jackie Kay

52. 1 mark for reference; 1 mark for comment (×2).

NB: Do not reward the same analytical comment given twice for two different references.

Possible answers include:

- "(Am a) burden (tae her)" suggests that the speaker is aware of her own dependency
- "Stuck (here)" suggests the speaker feels trapped
- "(big) blastit (bed)" suggests that the speaker is cursing the fact that she is confined to bed
- "big blastit bed" alliteration emphasises speaker's annoyance at being confined in bed
- "year in, year oot" repetition emphasises monotony/ endlessness of existence
- "ony saint wuid complain" suggests speaker's patience has been stretched
- "A' wish she didnae huv tae dae" suggests speaker's embarrassment at/awareness of dependency
- "(Am her) wean (noo)" suggests speaker feels she is treated like a baby/is dependent
- "ma great tent o' nappy" suggests speaker is embarrassed about undignified aspects of her current life
- "champed egg in a cup"/"mashed tattie" suggests speaker is critical of the food she has to eat/is given
- "Aw the treats…she's gieing me" suggests the speaker is unhappy about the role reversal with her daughter
- "A' dinny ken whit happened" suggests speaker's confusion over her current circumstances
- "We dinny talk any mair" suggests speaker's regret at loss of communication
- "the blethers ha been plucked oot o'us" suggests speaker is aware of lack of communication/ conversation

53. 1 mark for reference; 1 mark for comment (×2).

NB: Do not reward the same analytical comment given twice for two different references.

Possible answers include:

- "like some skinny chicken" suggests reduced physical state/loss of humanity or individuality
- "skinny" suggests weight loss
- "ma skin…loose flap noo" suggests skin is in poor condition
- "A' took pride in ma guid smooth skin" suggests contrast of current state of physical appearance with former state
- "Aw A' dae is sit an look oot this windae" suggests boredom
- "A've seen hale generations graw up" suggests being left behind
- "… this same windae" suggests length of time in one place/lack of variety
- "that's no seen a lick o' paint fir donkeys" suggests neglect

54. 1 mark for reference; 1 mark for comment.

Possible answers include:

- "so am telt"/"hauf the time A' dinny believe her" suggests lack of trust between mother and daughter
- "My dochter says 'Awright mother?'" suggests lack of genuine interest/concern from her daughter
- "(haunds me) a thin broth or puried neep" suggests speaker's unhappiness with the food her daughter brings her
- "an A say 'Aye fine,'" suggests response is not genuine
- "great heaving sigh"/"ma crabbit tut"/"ma froon"/"A' pu' ma cardie tight" suggests displeasure
- "ma auld loose lips" suggests speaking without thought

55. Two points for 1 mark each. Candidates should use their own words.

Gloss of:

- "biding time" e.g. waiting to die
- "Time is whit A' hauld between the soft bits o' ma thumbs" e.g. she knows that her time is limited/not much left
- "the skeleton underneath ma night goon" e.g. she is aware that death is approaching
- "the glaring selfish moon" e.g. she takes no joy from nature/the world
- "this drab wee prison" e.g. she feels trapped/lack of freedom
- "A'll be gone and how wull she feel" e.g. she has doubts over her daughter's emotions/attitude towards her
- "No that…Grateful" e.g. part of her wants her daughter to appreciate her more/her thoughts have become bitter

56. *Possible areas for comment include:*

- "Gap Year" — a mother reacting to/trying to adapt to her son having left home/being far away.
- "My Grandmother's Houses" — speaker reflects on the impact of moving house for her grandmother.
- "Lucozade" — change in relationships caused by illness/hospitalisation.
- "Divorce" — speaker desperately seeks change in relationship with parents.
- "Keeping Orchids" — speaker reflects on changing relationship with mother.

Candidates may choose to answer in **bullet points** in this final question, or write a number of linked statements. There is **no requirement** to write a "mini essay".

Up to 2 marks can be achieved for identifying elements of commonality as requested in the question. A further 2 marks can be achieved for **reference to the extract given**.

4 additional marks can be awarded for similar references to at **least one other poem by Kay**.

<u>In practice this means:</u>

Identification of commonality (e.g.: theme, central relationship, importance of setting, use of imagery, development in characterisation, use of personal experience, use of narrative style or any other key element...)

From the extract:

1 relevant reference to technique; 1 appropriate comment

OR 1 relevant reference to idea; 1 appropriate comment

OR 1 relevant reference to feature; 1 appropriate comment

OR 1 relevant reference to text; 1 appropriate comment

(maximum of 2 marks only for discussion of extract)

from at **least one other poem:**

as above (×2) for **up to 4 marks.**

SECTION 2 — CRITICAL ESSAY

Please see the assessment criteria for the Critical Essay on page 130.

Acknowledgements

Permission has been sought from all relevant copyright holders and Hodder Gibson is grateful for the use of the following:

An extract adapted from the article 'Missing penalty not end of world but a chance to learn more about life' by Matthew Syed © The Times/News Syndication, 9th July 2014 (2015 Reading for Understanding, Analysis and Evaluation pages 2 & 3);

An extract from 'Bold Girls' copyright © 1991 Rona Munro. Excerpted with permission of Nick Hern Books Ltd: www.nickhernbooks.co.uk (2015 Critical Reading pages 2 & 3);

An extract from 'Sailmaker' by Alan Spence. Reproduced by permission of Hodder Education (2015 Critical Reading page 4);

An extract from 'Tally's Blood' by Ann Marie di Mambro, published by Education Scotland. Reprinted by permission of Ann Marie di Mambro/MacFarlane Chard Associates (2015 Critical Reading pages 6 & 7);

An extract from 'The Cone-Gatherers' by Robin Jenkins, published by Canongate Books Ltd. (2015 Critical Reading page 8);

An extract from 'The Testament Of Gideon Mack' by James Robertson (Hamish Hamilton 2006, Penguin Books 2007). Copyright © James Robertson, 2006. Reproduced by permission of Penguin Books Ltd. (2015 Critical Reading pages 10 & 11);

An extract from 'Kidnapped' by Robert Louis Stevenson, published by Cassell and Company Ltd 1886. Public domain (2015 Critical Reading pages 12 & 13);

An extract from 'Mother and Son' by Iain Crichton Smith, taken from 'The Red Door: The Complete English Stories 1949–76', published by Birlinn. Reproduced with permission of Birlinn Limited via PLSclear (2015 Critical Reading page 14);

An extract from 'All that Glisters' by Anne Donovan, taken from 'Hieroglyphics and Other Stories', published by Canongate Books Ltd. (2015 Critical Reading page 16);

The poem 'Valentine' from 'Mean Time' by Carol Ann Duffy. Published by Anvil Press Poetry, 1993. Copyright © Carol Ann Duffy. Reproduced by permission of the author c/o Rogers, Coleridge & White Ltd., 20 Powis Mews, London W11 1JN (2015 Critical Reading page 18);

The poem 'Hyena' by Edwin Morgan, taken from 'From Glasgow to Saturn', published by Carcanet Press Limited 1973 (2015 Critical Reading pages 20 & 21);

The poem 'Visiting Hour' by Norman MacCaig, taken from 'The Poems of Norman MacCaig' edited by Ewan McCaig, published by Polygon. Reproduced with permission of Birlinn Limited via PLSclear (2015 Critical Reading page 22);

The poem 'Divorce' by Jackie Kay, from 'Darling: New & Selected Poems' (Bloodaxe Books, 2007). Reprinted with permission of Bloodaxe Books, on behalf of the author. www.bloodaxebooks.com (2015 Critical Reading page 24);

The article 'Can Idina Menzel ever Let It Go?' by Ed Potton © The Times/News Syndication, 6 February 2015 (2016 Reading for Understanding, Analysis and Evaluation pages 2 & 3);

An extract from 'Bold Girls' copyright © 1991 Rona Munro. Excerpted with permission of Nick Hern Books Ltd: www.nickhernbooks.co.uk (2016 Critical Reading pages 2 & 3);

An extract from 'Sailmaker' by Alan Spence. Reproduced by permission of Hodder Education (2016 Critical Reading pages 4 & 5);

An extract from 'Tally's Blood' by Ann Marie di Mambro, published by Education Scotland. Reprinted by permission of Ann Marie di Mambro/MacFarlane Chard Associates (2016 Critical Reading pages 6 & 7);

An extract from 'The Cone-Gatherers' by Robin Jenkins, published by Canongate Books Ltd. (2016 Critical Reading page 8);

An extract from 'The Testament Of Gideon Mack' by James Robertson (Hamish Hamilton 2006, Penguin Books 2007). Copyright © James Robertson, 2006. Reproduced by permission of Penguin Books Ltd. (2016 Critical Reading page 10);

An extract from 'Kidnapped' by Robert Louis Stevenson, published by Cassell and Company Ltd 1886. Public domain (2016 Critical Reading page 12);

An extract from 'The Painter' by Iain Crichton Smith, taken from 'The Red Door: The Complete English Stories 1949–76', published by Birlinn. Reproduced with permission of Birlinn Limited via PLSclear (2016 Critical Reading page 14);

An extract from 'Dear Santa' by Anne Donovan, taken from 'Hieroglyphics and Other Stories', published by Canongate Books Ltd. (2016 Critical Reading pages 16 & 17);

The poem 'Originally' by Carol Ann Duffy from 'The Other Country'. Published by Anvil Press Poetry, 1990. Copyright © Carol Ann Duffy. Reproduced by permission of the author c/o Rogers, Coleridge & White Ltd., 20 Powis Mews, London W11 1JN (2016 Critical Reading page 18);

The poem 'Good Friday' by Edwin Morgan, taken from 'New Selected Poems', published by Carcanet Press Limited 2000 (2016 Critical Reading page 20);